A SHORT HISTORY OF
ENGLISH LITERATURE

By the same Author:

Criticism and Biography

TRADITION AND ROMANTICISM

ENGLISH POETRY IN THE LATER NINETEENTH CENTURY

KEATS

THE POETRY OF WILLIAM MORRIS

ENGLISH LITERATURE BETWEEN THE WARS

A SHORT HISTORY OF ENGLISH DRAMA

Travel

ENCOUNTERS

Fiction

IN SEARCH OF STEPHEN VANE

THE SHOP ON THE KING'S ROAD

THE CHURCH IN THE MARKETS

Edited with W. W. Greg

THE COMEDY OF SUSANNA (*Malone Society*)

JACK JUGGLER (*Malone Society*)

A SHORT HISTORY OF ENGLISH LITERATURE

B. IFOR EVANS

S T A P L E S   P R E S S

STAPLES PRESS LIMITED
Mandeville Place, London

STAPLES PRESS INCORPORATED
70 East 45th Street, New York

First published as a 'PELICAN' *in* 1940

Revised Library Edition 1949
published by the courtesy of
'PENGUIN BOOKS LIMITED'

THIS BOOK IS SET IN
10 ON 11 POINT 'MONOTYPE' TIMES NEW ROMAN

Made and printed in England by
STAPLES PRESS LIMITED
at their Bayswater, London, establishment

TO

JOHN BERESFORD

CONTENTS

CHAPTER ONE

BEFORE THE CONQUEST

ENGLISH literature is often described as beginning with Chaucer. This would give England six centuries of literature. Actually there were more than six centuries of literature before Chaucer was born. The modern reader can make out the general meaning of a page of Chaucer without difficulty, but if he looks at our earliest writings he finds that they read like a foreign tongue. This is the reason for the neglect of our early literature, though today much of it can be obtained in translation.

The two most important events in the history of England took place before the Norman Conquest. It was in that period that the Angles and Saxons and Jutes came to England in marauding bands and made English history possible. From all accounts they were respectable gentlemen when at home, but they changed their manners when they were looking for *Lebensraum*. They were heathen, and the second great event at that time was the conversion of the English to Christianity. In 597 Augustine had come from Rome and begun to convert the Jutes in Kent, while about the same time monks from Ireland were setting up monasteries in Northumbria. Most English poetry in the early Anglo-Saxon period is associated with these two events. Either the stories are brought over by the invading tribes from their continental Germanic homes, or they are Christian stories.

Literature in the Anglo-Saxon period was recorded in manuscripts, and the life of a manuscript is a hard one. Our knowledge of Anglo-Saxon poetry depends on four groups of manuscripts. These are: the manuscripts collected by Sir Robert Cotton, which are now in the British Museum; the Exeter Book given to Exeter Cathedral by Bishop Leofric, some time after 1050; the Vercelli Book, found at Vercelli, near

Milan in 1822 (and no one has given a satisfactory account of how it got there); and finally the manuscripts in the Bodleian Library at Oxford, given by the Dutch scholar Francis Dujon or Junius, Librarian to the Earl of Arundel. In Sir Robert Cotton's collection is the manuscript of *Beowulf*, the most important poem of the Anglo-Saxon period, and its history shows how everything seems to fight against the possibilities of a manuscript surviving.

The Angles brought the story of *Beowulf* with them to England in the sixth century, and there somewhere about A.D. 700 the poem was made. This was about seventy years after the death of Mohammed and in the same age as the beginning of the great Tang Dynasty in China. Three hundred years later, about the year 1000, the manuscript, which still survives, was written down. What happened to it for the next seven hundred years is unknown. In 1706 it was recorded as being in Sir Robert Cotton's library. Only twenty-six years later a disastrous fire broke out in the library, and only narrowly did it escape. The charred edges of the leaves can still be seen in the manuscript now preserved in the British Museum. Two fragments of another poem, *Waldere*, which may originally have been as long as *Beowulf*, were found as recently as 1860 in the binding of a book in the Royal Library at Copenhagen.

The hero and the setting of *Beowulf*, the first long poem in English, have nothing to do with England. Though the Angles brought the story to England, it is not even about the Angles, but about the Scandinavians. The German tribes, though they warred with each other, and with anyone else within reach, had a 'free trade' in stories. Their poets, at least, believed in 'Germania', the single German people. So it is that our first English poem is a Scandinavian story, brought over by the Angles, and made into a poem in England. The story of *Beowulf* is of a monster named Grendel who is disturbing Hrothgar, king of the Danes, in Heorot, his great hall. A young warrior called Beowulf comes with a group of comrades to the rescue. He overcomes Grendel and then later in a dwelling at the bottom of a lake he fights Grendel's mother, a sea monster. In the second part of the poem Beowulf is a king, and as an old of St. Juliana; *Elene*, or the story of the finding of the Cross by St. Helena; the *Fates of the Apostles* and a poem on Christ's Ascension.

Whoever wrote the other religious poems on biblical themes or on saints' lives, three remain of outstanding quality. One is part of the Genesis story, the account of the Fall of the Angels, known as *Genesis B*. The English poet, using an Old Saxon poem, has made a vivid rendering of the story which Milton was later to tell in *Paradise Lost*. The Anglo-Saxon poet has admirable art in his portrayal of the character of Satan and of the geography of Hell. The second is *The Dream of the Rood*, by far the most imaginative of the Old English poems. The Cross appears to the poet in a dream and describes the unwilling part it played in the Crucifixion. The third is the story of *Judith*, the most exciting narrative in Anglo-Saxon poetry and told with realism. It tells the Apocryphal story of how Judith slew the tyrant Holofernes. Nothing in Anglo-Saxon poetry approaches *Judith* in its dramatic quality or in the sense it gives of genuine human characterization.

The personalities who make the prose of the Anglo-Saxon period can be seen more clearly. The earliest definite figure is Aldhelm (*d.* 709) bishop of Sherborne, who wrote praises of virginity in an ornate Latin. The greatest figure is the Venerable Bede (672-735), who spent nearly the whole of his life of intense study in the monastery at Jarrow. He never travelled farther than from Jarrow to York, but his mind travelled over all the studies then known, history, astronomy, saints' lives, and the suffering of the martyrs. Foremost among his works is his great *Ecclesiastical History of the English Race*. He made his monastery at Jarrow a centre of civilization in that troubled century when the Christian civilization of Europe was threatened with destruction. His own life seems to have had a beauty and simplicity such as the Irish monks had brought into their settlements in England; but in him this simplicity was combined with an outstanding quality of mind. Bede wrote in Latin and the excellence of his work gave him in his own lifetime a European reputation, which lasted long after his death.

In the century after Bede, the Danish invasion broke up a

nascent civilization in England. One after another the great abbey houses were destroyed. It is strange how often a nation's hour of trial produces a great figure. Such was England's fortune when, in 871, a young man of twenty-two became king. Alfred (849-901) deserves to be remembered as one of the outstanding figures in our history. Soldier, strategist, scholar, educator, administrator. Above all he was a personality most resourceful and courageous, who played the Danes with appeasement until he was ready to meet them. He was not only the military saviour of his people. He had a zest for knowledge and for the distribution of knowledge. Much of his work was translation and much of it he only directed, but in all, his was the guiding spirit. As a manual for the instruction of the clergy he prepared a translation of the *Pastoral Rule* of Gregory the Great. So that his people might know their own country better he began the translation of Bede's *Ecclesiastical History*. He also had translated the *History of the World*, of Orosius, the H. G. Wells of this early period, not nearly as interesting as is Wells, but very popular. Alfred touched up Orosius with the accounts given him by two travellers, Ohthere and Wulfstan, of 'Germania' and the countries beyond its boundaries. Nothing shows Alfred's enquiring mind more clearly than his desire to have these accounts of contemporary travellers inserted into Orosius's dull chronicle of calamities. If Orosius's work was prepared for the instruction of his people, Boethius's *Consolation of Philosophy* he rendered to please himself. Writing in prison Boethius had proved that the only genuine happiness comes from the spirit, from an inward serenity, and Alfred found something in his own life to answer this mood. One other work Alfred inspired. Out of the narratives of contemporary events, kept by the monasteries, he conceived the idea of a national history, and this for a time was achieved in the *Anglo-Saxon Chronicle*. The work as a whole is by a number of hands, of varying skill. It continues after Alfred's death, and the Peterborough version has records to the year 1154. The account of the wars with the Danes shows how many suffered in that age, how bitter, insecure, and cruel life was. When one thinks of Alfred with that as his background, his stature as a man increases, until he towers up as one of the great figures of our history.

In the century after his death much of the work he had begun was lost, but two writers, both of them monks of the strict order of St. Benedict, wrote a religious prose which has been preserved. Aelfric, a pupil of the monastery school at Winchester, and a teacher in the Abbey at Cerne Abbas, constructed homilies in English so that 'unlettered' men might be made more ready to meet their God. His language is rhythmical and elaborate, and its effects more like that of verse than that of the more direct and practical prose of Alfred. The other memorable writer is Wulfstan, Archbishop of York, whose *A Sermon of the Wulf* was addressed to the English, 'when the Danes were persecuting them most severely.' Wulfstan makes a flaming indictment of Aethelred, a weak and cowardly king, of unpreparedness in defence, of villages destroyed, of moral and national disintegration. Wulfstan confirms the accounts in the *Chronicle* of the cruelty and hopelessness of the years of the Danish invasion. Aelfric in one of his prefaces told his readers that the end of the world was at hand. Not that, just yet, but the end of the Anglo-Saxon world.

CHAPTER TWO

ENGLISH POETRY FROM CHAUCER TO JOHN DONNE

EACH art has its own medium: the painter his pigments, the musician his sounds, and the writer, words. The difficulty of the writer is that words are used for all everyday purposes, so that they become worn, like coins rubbed by long use. The poet, more than any other writer, tries to look at words afresh. In a poem he so arranges words, that they give pleasure such as we may have from music or from pictures. Much of that pleasure derives from the words themselves, but part of it comes from their rhythmical arrangement. The order of the words is such that their sounds please, while the alternations of accent and time give to a verbal pattern some of the pleasure which music gives. The poet, compared with the musician, is faced with the added difficulty that words in their normal use convey a meaning. The musician is not controlled by a meaning and some poets have tried to rid themselves of this embarrassment. They wish to create patterns and rhythms disembodied from meaning. At the same time most of the great poets have regarded meaning as of primary importance. They have used poetry to express their knowledge of love, death, and of their aspirations. They have also used poetry to tell stories, the comedy, the pathos, and the tragedy of life.

Modern poetry begins with Geoffrey Chaucer (1340-1400), diplomat, soldier, and scholar. He was a *bourgeois* who understood the Court and had a keen eye for the ordinary man, and he was a reader who had studied most of the literature available at his time. More particularly, he profited by his French and Italian journeys to study the more ambitious ways of continental poetry. Like every scholar of his time he knew medieval Latin, and he had read diligently some of the Latin classics, especially Ovid and Vergil. He wrote because he must have been aware of his own genius. His audience was necessarily a small one, and in his own life-time could not have been more than a few thousand people, comprising courtiers, and members of the rising professional and merchant classes.

Much in his work shows his taste for medieval literature, particularly as it was found in France. He delighted in allegory, and in the elaborate sentiments of courtly love. Even if he is not the author of the translation of *The Romance of the Rose* of Guillaume de Lorris and the satirical Jean de Meung, he had studied their poem closely. Guillaume had treated woman with adoration, and Jean with mockery, and Chaucer remembered both ways in his own verses. His more completely medieval poems are represented by *The Book of the Duchess* (1369), an allegory on the death of Blanche, wife of John of Gaunt, and *The House of Fame*, a dream medley with some classical memories but full of intricate and sometimes rambling medieval lore. These, with his lyrics, the ballades, and rondels, would have made him a considerable poet for his century, but three other works set him apart as a great poet in the history of poetry in general. These three works are: *Troilus and Criseyde* (1385-7), *The Legend of Good Women* (1385), and the unfinished *Canterbury Tales*.

Of these, the most ambitious as a complete work is *Troilus and Criseyde*. The story, which Shakespeare later used in the most difficult of his plays, Chaucer had found in Boccaccio's *Il Filostrato*. It was a medieval addition to the classical theme of the Trojan wars, the story of Troilus's love for Criseyde and of her faithlessness. The story would do for a novel, and in some ways Chaucer has made a great novel in verse, with characters intelligible in any age, and with a full movement of life surrounding the main theme. His characterization is distinct, not only of the lovers themselves, but of Pandarus, Criseyde's uncle, the comic, friendly sensual go-between, whose comments and wit make him the first fully-drawn figure in our literature. In comparison *The Legend of Good Women* seems a slight piece, with its brief narratives of the unhappy fate of Cleopatra, Thisbe, Philomela and others, who suffered in the cause of love. In the *Prologue* to this poem Chaucer returned to allegory, to the medieval Garden of the Rose, and embedded in this part of the poem is the most beautiful of all his lyrics, 'Hide, Absalon, thy giltė tresses clear.'

It is for the *Canterbury Tales* that Chaucer's name is best remembered, the unfinished collection of stories told by the pilgrims on their journey to Canterbury, with the *Prologue*, the clearest picture of late medieval life existent anywhere. His quick, sure strokes portray the pilgrims at once as types and individuals true of their own age and, still more, representative of humanity in general. The idea of a collection of stories Chaucer may have had from Boccaccio's *Decameron*, but he borrowed little more than the initial idea. He keeps the whole poem alive by interspersing the tales themselves with the talk, the quarrels, and the opinions of the pilgrims, and here the Wife of Bath with her detailed comments on marriage and the treatment of the male sex is supreme.

How great was Chaucer's art can be seen by comparing his work with that of John Gower (1325-1408), who shared many of Chaucer's interests, and if Chaucer had not lived, Gower would be one of the outstanding poets remembered from this century. Like Chaucer he read French and Latin as easily as he read English, and he composed poems with equal fluency in all three languages.

In Chaucer's age the English language was still divided by dialects, though London was rapidly making East-Midland into a standard language. In the West there lived on, or came to life, a poetry which has little in common with that of Chaucer, and which he seems to have actively disliked. Outstanding is the *The Vision of Piers the Plowman*, by William Langland. I write William Langland, though some have divided him into five, but the plastic surgery of modern English scholarship seems to be putting him together again. The author was probably a priest of one of the lower orders, and his poem may have circulated among clerical or semi-clerical audiences. The number of extant manuscripts shows that the poem was popular, and the author's own continued interest in his work is proved by his three versions: the A version of 1362, the B, or main, version of 1377, and C, the longest, of 1395. The poem begins with a Vision, which the poet had on the Malvern Hills, of a 'field full of folk.' In a long and complicated succession of scenes he portrays almost every side of fourteenth-century life. He sees the corruption of wealth, and the inadequacies of government. To him the only salvation lies in honest labour and in the service of Christ. If he were not a mystic he would be a revolutionary. He is the nearest approach to Dante in our poetry, for despite his roughness and the bleak atmosphere of much of his work he has written the greatest poem in English devoted to the Christian way of life.

Nor was Langland's poem the only one which came out of the West Country. A single manuscript preserves four poems written in the North-Western dialect. *Pearl*, *Purity*, *Patience*, and *Gawain and the Green Knight*, have sufficient similarities to lead some to the belief that they were all the work of one author. *Pearl*, the outstanding religious poem of the group, is of a father who has lost his child, and the mystical language describing his vision has the glamour and fervour of the Book of Revelation.

Sir Gawain is the most subtle verse romance in English medieval literature. The romances, the stories of Arthur, of Charlemagne, and of the Trojan Wars and the more native stories of *King Horn* and *Havelock the Dane*, are among the most typical products of medieval literature, but not now the most interesting. Chaucer thought poorly of them at their worst, as is shown in his satire of *Sir Thopas*. The romances miss human life and character, and these elements *Gawain*, despite the incredible story, is able to supply in the descriptions of hunting, and in the scenes of Gawain's temptation.

Compared with the romances, the life of the medieval lyric has been strong and enduring. The tunes, and the phrasing of many of the lyrics which survive, especially those in the famous Harleian Manuscript 2253, come to the ear with an unsullied freshness:

Between March and Averil
When spray beginneth to spring.

Best of all the medieval lyrics is *Alysoun*, which survives every change in the language, and remains today perfect and unmatchable.

With the lyrics may be remembered the ballads, for the ballads were lyrics in which a story was told in one particular way. Possibly the ballads are the part of medieval literature which has survived the best. *Sir Patrick Spens* and *The Mill Dams of Binnorie* have all the magic which later generations were to associate with the Middle Ages. Further, they possess a way of verse, subtle and allusive, which is not to be found elsewhere in these centuries.

Chaucer as a poet is so good that he makes the fifteenth century appear dull. His imitators are brought on to the stage of literature only to receive cat-calls from the critics. So it is with Thomas Occleve, and with John Lydgate, though the latter cannot at least be accused of indolence. Actually no one did imitate the best in Chaucer. Lydgate and the others are far better judged independently for what they attempted to do. Lydgate is a translator, and at least he made available in English a large number of stories and romances. The poets of the century after Chaucer were involved further in the changing nature of our language, especially in the loss of the final 'e', which made unrhythmical a line which, pronounced as Chaucer pronounced it, had a free and regular beauty.

The more elaborate poets seem imitative and repetitive. One feels that poetry must have some new voice, however sharp and discordant. The situation is not unlike that at the end of the Victorian age. One tradition has gone on too long. It must be dispersed before poetry can redevelop. Of this older tradition the allegories of Stephen Hawes, especially *The Pastime of Pleasure*, are typical. They seem to belong to a dead past. One poet in this age by his rude originality served to emphasize this wraith-like quality of Hawes and the courtly imitators of Chaucer. John Skelton (1460?-1529) wrote a ragged, uncouth line, broken, irregular, but compact with meaning, and brutal in its directness:

Though my rime be ragged,
Tatter'd and jagged,

Rudely rain-beaten,
Rusty and moth-eaten,
If ye take well therewith,
It hath in it some pith.

He is satiric, pungent, foul-mouthed, but after the endless diet of allegorical sweet-meats even the deliberate absence of beauty in his verse is pleasing. Skelton could also write in another way with gentleness and poignancy as is to be heard in his *Book of Philip Sparrow* on the death of a favourite sparrow.

In Scotland, Chaucer fared better, with Robert Henryson's *Testament of Cresseid*, and with a royal supporter in King James I of Scotland's *Kingis Quair*. William Dunbar belongs to the same school, but he is too original to be described as an imitator; the colour and elaborate device of his verse seem like some medieval tourney come to life again, or like a heraldic device set into words. With these the text-books have always put Gavin Douglas, and so that the four may not be separated his name is added here. If his own verse is unexceptional, this 'humanist in verse,' as Andrew Lang once called him is best remembered for his rendering of Vergil into English verse.

The new way in English poetry came mainly through the imitation of Italian models and it brought difficulties of its own. The early stages of this Italian influence can be found in poems by Wyatt and Surrey published in 1557 in an anthology generally known as *Tottel's Miscellany*. Wyatt and Surrey have so often been grouped together in histories of literature that they seem almost as inseparably linked as the names of two drapers. Yet they are distinct and memorable personalities. Sir Thomas Wyatt was a courtier and diplomat who kept his head, in more than one sense of the word, in the troubled Court of Henry VIII, and the Earl of Surrey was a nobleman who went to the scaffold at the age of thirty. Wyatt, who could write graceful and sad-toned lyrics successfully, when he was not thinking of Italian models, struggled to render into English the fourteen-line Italian form of the sonnet. He succeeded, but the marks of the painful signs of the difficulties he encountered are upon his verses. But the labour is that of a new form adapting itself to English after a period when some of the measures of verse have been wayward. Surrey, who seemed to compose with less apparent effort, also practised the sonnet, though the most important of his experiments was the translation of the second and fourth books of Vergil's *Aeneid* into English blank verse. Surrey can little have guessed how honourable would be the heritage of the measure which he was employing. Introduced here for the first time into English as a medium for translating from the Latin, blank verse was to become, through Marlowe's employment, the great measure of English poetic drama, to be used by Shakespeare, and by other verse dramatists to the present day. In non-dramatic verse the lineage was no less noble: Milton chose it for *Paradise Lost*, Keats for *Hyperion*, Tennyson for the *Idylls*, and many other poets have found within it a method for narrative, discourse, and satire.

Nor could Wyatt and Surrey have known how often the sonnet form would attract later poets. They themselves, influenced by Petrarch, used the sonnet for love poems of a particular type: the lover is dutiful, anxious, adoring, of wanhope, and full of praises of his mistress couched in a series of conventionalized images; the mistress is proud, unreceptive, but, if the lover is to be believed, very desirable. Throughout the Elizabethan age, poets imitated these Petrarchan moods of love, and used the sonnet to express them. Some saw through the artificialities of the sentiment, which Shakespeare mocked with the speeches of Mercutio in *Romeo and Juliet*. Sir Philip Sidney, in *Astrophel and Stella*, jested at the fashion, and yet half succumbed to it: some of his sonnets plead for realism, and others luxuriate in the baroque devices which the convention allowed. Shakespeare, though he satirized sonnet-writing, was himself a sonneteer, and his volume of sonnets has brought forth more discussion than any other single work of literary composition in the language. As always, Shakespeare is different. Some of his sonnets are addressed not to a woman but to a young man, and they are in the terms of warmest affection. Others are written not with adoration but with an air of disillusioned passion to a 'dark lady.' His power over words, from the play of the pun to the very transmutation of speech, marks them all. The pretty things are there, but with them a profound moral vision in the graver sonnets.

The sonnet outlived the Elizabethan period. For whatever changes come over the fashion of writing from time to time, poets have returned to the compact fourteen lines, which are more than merely fourteen lines, for they constitute a unity of poetic speech. Milton used the sonnet, not however for amorous dainties, but to define moments of autobiography, and for brief, powerful comments on public events. To the sonnet Wordsworth returned to awaken England from lethargy, to condemn Napoleon, and to record many of his own moods. Keats, who had studied Shakespeare and Milton to such purpose, discovered himself as a poet in his sonnet, *On First Looking into Chapman's Homer.* In the nineteenth century Meredith in *Modern Love* showed how the sonnet, modified to a poem of sixteen lines, could be made a vehicle of analysis, and D. G. Rossetti in *The House of Life* came back, though with many changes, to the older way of Dante and Petrarch, employing this most perfect of all miniature verse forms for the expression of love.

Wyatt and Surrey are greater in the traditions which they started than in the poetry which they themselves produced. They were succeeded by Edmund Spenser (1552-99), who was a master of the poetic art, and was acknowledged by his contemporaries as a master. Of his life little is known. He was an undergraduate at Cambridge, and liked by the elegant and the clever, including Gabriel Harvey (1545-1630), whom the young men of those days regarded as the wisest of their elders. No one in his family could help him in the painful road that led from the University to the Court. His art made him some friends, and his intelligence others. Possibly his personality helped, though of this little is known. The Earl of Leicester chose him for his service, and he followed Leicester to Ireland and the scenery of that country, and some of the cruelty he witnessed are reflected indirectly in *The Faerie Queene*. Except for two visits to England, he lived in Ireland until his death in

1599. Among his poems, two volumes at least will always be remembered, though possibly with many they are now only remembered as names. *The Shepherd's Calendar* of 1579 and *The Faerie Queene*, which began publication in 1590.

Spenser, like most great artists, felt the form and pressure of his time conditioning his writing. He was aware of a desire to make English a fine language, full of magnificent words, with its roots in the older and popular traditions of the native tongue. He had the ambition to write in English, poems which would be great and revered, as the classical epics of Homer and Vergil had been, or the new ambitious romantic poetry of Ariosto and Tasso. He was aware of the popular stories and myths, which had lingered on from the Middle Ages, the Arthurian tales, the allegories, the giants, and enchanters. He knew, no less, the nobly-fashioned heroic tales from the classical world, of Hector and Achilles, Ulysses, and Aeneas. Somehow he would make a poem in which the medley of native story joined with a classical ambition in presentation. Double, even treble, motives crossed within his mind, all ultimately controlled by the fact that his surest audience lay within the Court, his most treasured auditor, if only she would listen, the Queen herself, Gloriana, the Faerie Queene. His mind looked out beyond the Court to the people, to their superstitions and faiths, and he had even the grave moral aim of improving the England which he loved, but the Court and the Queen were in the forefront of his vision. In him the medieval and renaissance meet, the modern and the classical, the courtly and popular.

Whatever may have been the perplexity of these aims, he remained an artist. Words fascinated him, their shape, and colour, and above all their rhythmical arrangement. His early work, *The Shepherd's Calendar*, may have lost much of the freshness which it had in 1579, but one can read again the April eclogue and succumb to the music of the words, as one must in the later poems of *Prothalamion* and *Epithalamion*. This is the final effect of *The Faerie Queene*, a wash made from the brightest pigments, with little to arrest the intellect or astound the imagination, as with Shakespeare. The stanza, which Spenser invented for *The Faerie Queene*, has this miraculous power of gathering words up into itself, caressingly, and so adorning them with its music that they become more notable than they ever were before.

All this may be said justly without ever reinstating Spenser as a popular poet. *The Shepherd's Calendar*, read for the first time, is an odd, difficult, and old-fashioned work. It cannot be judged straight from human experience, as can Chaucer's *Troilus and Criseyde*. Like a museum piece it needs a reference to the catalogue, before its virtues can be appreciated. Spenser has written twelve 'eclogues,' or shepherd's poems, one for each month of the year, and, in the manner of the classical and renaissance eclogue-writer, permitted himself a variety of themes, from satire on the church to praise of the Queen. The title promises a simple rustic book, but the poems are clever, mock-simple, courtly pieces. They represent, nothing more clearly, the duality of Spenser's mind.

The Faerie Queene, a poem which has attracted most English poets since Spenser's time, is not likely now to be a popular one. To see it in this twentieth century is like finding an apartment appointed with steel furniture hung with a faded tapestry of the Masque of Cupid; or to see Arthur or Gawain appear, wraith-like, on some dirt-track racing course. Even in that Elizabethan age this poem spoke of a past, fast fading, but still remembered. Spenser had chosen from the medieval romances, and particularly the Arthurian stories, a medley of narrative which he could weave into a series of allegorical adventures. The allegory itself now seems troublesome, but to the Elizabethans it had a contemporary reference, and they were near enough to the Middle Ages to devour allegory for its own sake. Above all, the modern mind, with its craving for realism, will miss the human figures, which Chaucer and Shakespeare supply.

Little read though the poem may now be, it has had its influence not on our literature only, but in some indirect way on the English temper itself. The 'courtesy' of the Middle Ages, the romantic sentiment, idealized by Spenser in the ceremony of marriage, are here embodied in our literature, and they are part of our own civilized attitude to life. Further, when the world of commerce was about to lay its ugly and contaminating fingers on life, here is a poem, enshrining with security, a world unstained by any commercial value. The reader may give thanks for the mysterious working on the English spirit in a poem which he has left unread. Unread it will be as a poem. But those who wander in Arabia record amid the arid places sudden sights which repay the labour of their journeys and so it is with *The Faerie Queene*; the whole poem may weary, yet in the show passages, such as the Bower of Bliss, and the Masque of Cupid, it can still give warm, ample, and unhurried delight.

The best poetry of the Elizabethan age went into the drama, and, apart from Spenser, no one can compare with Marlowe and Shakespeare as writers of verse. The dramatists proved themselves poets outside the drama: Marlowe with *Hero and Leander*, Shakespeare with *Venus and Adonis*, *Lucrece*, and the *Sonnets*, and Ben Jonson with numerous lyrics, including the well-known, *Drink to me only with thine eyes*. Yet poetry flourished in that time, and the poems varied from long Colossus-like pieces to the most delicate songs and lyrics. The work of Michael Drayton (1563-1631), a representative poet, is a museum of most of the ways in which poetry could then be written. He was unmoved by the Italian romantic epics, which had encouraged Spenser's genius, but almost every other way of poetry he attempted. He could erect poetic Leviathans, and he could turn a lyric, as light as a feather blown into the sunlight. His historical poem, *The Barons' Wars* (1603), moves at a steady pace. Its sluggish treatment of the material illustrates by contrast what a powerful imagination Shakespeare employed when he converted history into genuine poetic drama. Heavy though it is, it becomes insubstantial when compared with the huge body of the *Polyolbion*, where using the long alexandrine line Drayton conducts the reader in many thousand lines through the geography of England. Unread, but not unreadable, the poem had one motive in common with *The Faerie Queene*, for, as a whole, it was a love of England that led Drayton to gather into his seemingly unending narrative, legends, beliefs, and descriptions illustrating English life. But Drayton could turn from these ponderous works to compose *Nymphidia*, the happiest of our fairy poems; the compact and stirring *Ballad of Agincourt*, and that admirable sonnet, 'Since there's no help,' for which many would sacrifice much of the rest of his work.

Samuel Daniel (1562-1619) had something of the same energy in composition, combined with the same absence of dominating diction. Like Drayton, he attempted to write history in verse with *The Civil Wars between Lancaster and York* (1595-1609), but his most genuine talent lay in reflective poetry, which, in poems such as his *Epistles*, was later to attract Wordsworth's attention.

The longer poems of the Elizabethan age demand concessions from the reader. He must approach them with an historical interest, or his taste will be offended and his attention diverted. But the songs and lyrics, in which the age delighted, have ever been the delight of posterity. Shakespeare, in *Twelfth Night*, shows how in the house of the Duke Orsino the song was a ready and acceptable entertainment. So it was in the great houses of the Elizabethans, and in the Court of the Queen herself. Many of the poets of that age knew the art of wedding verse and sounds, and in the song-books of the period can be found the lyrics of Thomas Campion, and others who had delighted the audiences of their day.

One has to stretch across the years to reach Drayton and Daniel, but John Donne (1573-1631) seems often to stand before us as a contemporary. His life was adventurous, a gallant, a courtier, a member of Essex's Cadiz expedition, secretary to the Lord Keeper, a prisoner for his runaway match with his master's niece, and at length the Dean of St. Paul's. His mind was restless and adventurous: he read widely, treasuring the most recondite forms of knowledge. Some intense nervous excitement marked all that he thought, all that he did. He had the power of experiencing keenly, and of reviewing the experience against the background of quite contrary moods. He is the lover and the sensualist, but his mind reviews his love in the terms of philosophy, or explores it with the images gathered in his scientific and theological reading. He can perceive beauty, but at the very moment of that perception he sees the corpse, the cerement cloths, the skeleton. He knows passion, but he can mock at the physical body through which passion is transmitted. This restlessness brings his mind and his body very close to each other. His thought is ever at the service of his passions; his passions enter into his thought. Contraries exist in his mind, but they are ever moving one into the other. He is the young gallant who ends his life as Dean of St Paul's.

This frankness in passion, this despair of making a unity out of the broken images of life, have brought him close to some contemporary poets. He was naturally impatient of the conventional verse forms, of the regular rhythms, the well-worn similes. Instead of the accepted catalogue of comparisons used by the Petrarchan sonneteers, he sought out the strangest images. Dr Johnson, borrowing the term from Dryden, was later to name him and his school the 'metaphysical' poets, because they yoked ideas which no one had yet seen together. That Donne did this is true, but often he can achieve his effects in another way, by the most brief and simple of statements, and though not a mystic he is 'metaphysical' in the true philosophical sense in a way Johnson would not allow.

A 'school' of poets Donne certainly created, and much of the history of poetry in the seventeenth century could be written in the terms of loyalty or antagonism to his manner. His most interesting followers were religious poets. George Herbert (1593-1633), compared with Donne, has a simple and unimpeded devoutness. Yet the lyrics in *The Temple* successfully employ an unusual, often a homely, imagery, to give expression to religious experience. Henry Vaughan (1622-95), who was influenced by Donne and Herbert, had a mysticism which is recorded in poems such as *The Retreat*, and in *I saw Eternity the other Night*, but not all his work reaches their high level. The third of this group was Richard Crashaw (1572-1626), the Catholic poet, whose *Steps to the Temple* (1646) shows the influence not only of Donne but of Marini, the Italian poet, who used similarly elaborate forms.

Among the poets who had written verses lamenting the death of Donne had been Thomas Carew (1598-1639), one of the earliest of the 'Cavalier' poets. His verses had grace and wit, and his love lyrics and madrigals have found a place in the anthologies. His long poem, *The Rapture*, has not been similarly honoured, for, whatever may be its poetical merit, it has a licentiousness of which anthologists do not normally approve. Carew was the most careful of these 'Cavalier' lyrists, some of whom appear to be brilliant amateurs in verse. Sir John Suckling (1609-42), though he wrote often and sometimes seriously, seems to have been improvising in some of his light and cynical love lyrics. Richard Lovelace (1618-58) had probably a less sustained poetic gift than either Carew or Suckling, but he had the good fortune to make a few happily-turned songs, including *Stone walls do not a prison make*, by which his name will be remembered. A little apart from these 'Cavalier' lyrists was Ben Jonson's disciple Robert Herrick (1591-1674), who spent his exile as a cleric in Devonshire in the composition of verses. His poems were collected in 1648 as *Hesperides*, a volume which contains over a hundred pieces, both secular and divine. Less conscious in his verse than Ben Jonson, he had learnt from his master the art of brief expression, and to this he added his own lyrical gift, and his power of seizing upon the illuminating but unexpected word. The whole of the English countryside in its May-days and fairings and its half-pagan rustic ritual comes to life in his poems. The lyrics are often of love, fanciful, light-hearted, but with a gentle melancholy as he remembers how swiftly the joys of the earth disappear. While Herrick lived in retirement, Andrew Marvell (1621-78) was close to the great life of his country in the troubled days of the Commonwealth and the Restoration. He was himself on the Puritan side, and his poems after the return of Charles II are satiric and filled with an angry bitterness. They contrast in a marked way with his early verses, where nature and contemplation and retirement unite in a lyrical poetry which is at once gentle and strong.

CHAPTER THREE

ENGLISH POETRY FROM MILTON TO WILLIAM BLAKE

THE seventeenth century is in many ways the century of transition into our modern world. The Civil Wars separated men from the older ways of living, and the religious controversies killed much that had remained lively in the national imagination since the Middle Ages. The blight of commercialism, soon to be followed by industry, was setting its ugly plague upon the features of magnificence. Science, and, with Science, rationalism were growing in power, and much of that power was to be used to destroy man's capacity for myth-making, to remove from the arts much of the authority they had once possessed. Donne's restlessness seems the anticipation of a sensitive personality feeling not so much with his mind as with the 'tips of his fingers' the world which is to arise around him. A few of his followers, such as Abraham Cowley (1618-67), accepted the new situation with a facile optimism, believing that somehow science and poetry could be employed each in the service of the other.

It was in this period, when the position of the poet had been made difficult, that John Milton (1608-74) wrote in a manner that recalled poetry to the most elevated and regal conception of its function. His early work was written before the Civil Wars, and included *Comus* (1634), and many of the minor poems which were first collected in 1645. In the national upheaval he was occupied as a controversialist and Latin Secretary, and those who know Milton only from his verse may well be surprised to discover the vituperation and abuse which he dealt out to his opponents in the pamphleteering warfare. In the Civil Wars Milton supported what was ultimately the losing side, and the disappointment was the more severe as the cause of Cromwell had awakened in him high hopes for the future of humanity. A gesture of the heroic marked his closing years, when blind, half-fugitive, old, hope-shattered, he turned to compose the great poetic works which from his youth had haunted his imagination. *Paradise Lost* was published in 1667; *Paradise Regained* and *Samson Agonistes* in 1671.

Of Milton's works *Comus* is probably the most popular and intelligible today. Those who have seen the piece played will not be led away by the text-book disquisitions on its dramatic ineffectiveness. Like some other plays, it reads badly but acts well, and the fact that it is not very like a masque needs trouble only the pedant. As far as *Comus* has a story it tells of the temptation of the chaste maiden by the enchanter Comus, and of the power which her virtue gave her to resist him. Almost all the ideas that govern Milton's later poetry are already here. He saw life as a struggle, the Puritan struggle, for the survival of the good and the virtuous. So Eve and Adam were told to contend in *Paradise Lost*, so does Christ struggle against Satan in *Paradise Regained*, and Samson against false counsels in *Samson Agonistes*.

For Milton this struggle is never easy, for his mind is aware of the attractions of the earth and the pleasures of the body; to Comus he gives a magnificent plea that all the pleasures of the earth should be enjoyed. While the Puritan ideal was not easy, still less was it negative. It is regrettable that he composed his later and mature works when circumstances had cast such a black shadow across his path. No one who moves among these later poems can fail to feel the chill which blows around their massive colonnades, inducing a sense of loneliness, and a desire for ordinary human companionship. Yet they are amongst the greatest of our non-dramatic poems. The story of Adam and Eve may have ceased to have much importance for most minds, and this tells against Milton. Nothing can destroy the picture of Satan's rebellion, half-heroic, half-evil, or the language which seeks over human experience and past literature, for parallels to describe this cosmic action. He had from the first a sense of dedication to poetry, as he has himself expressed in *Lycidas*, and his whole mental life became a discipline so that he might achieve the great poems which in his youth he had outlined in his imagination.

If Milton showed Puritanism at its best, Samuel Butler (1612-80), in his satire *Hudibras*, exposed all the hypocrisies of Puritanism, and its cramping of the human spirit. In this burlesque poem, through which moves the spirit of Cervantes, he shows great comic intention in displaying the Presbyterian knight Sir Hudibras and his squire, Ralph, in action. Beneath the comedy and the coarseness there seems to dwell a cynical, perhaps a sceptical, mind. The poem was popular at the time, and it can be still enjoyed. The contrast of this intelligent buffoonery with Milton's grand manner is complete.

The legend that Milton was an unpopular poet has lived so long that probably it will never be destroyed. The facts cry out against the legend; he was read in his own age, and throughout the eighteenth century he was imitated widely though never very intelligently. He has always been read since by that minority which finds pleasure in poetry as an art, and the attempt in the twentieth century by some younger critics to attack Milton is as unjust as it is misinstructed. It is true that in his own age he stood, somewhat deliberately, apart, and that poetry followed other ways. The clearest 'movement' in Milton's age came from those who desired a greater simplicity in verse, with the employment of contemporary and intelligible themes. Those who believed in this manner developed the use of one particular form of verse known as the heroic couplet. It is the type of verse which later Pope was to make famous:

True ease in writing comes from art, not chance,
As those move easiest who have learn'd to dance.

Neat, measured, exact, regular, the heroic couplet was like a rococo façade, and the complete contrast to the twisted, agonized lines in which Donne tortured himself into expression. The beginning of this 'regular' movement has always been associated with the names of Edmund Waller (1606-87), and Sir John Denham (1615-69). That the changes which they made in poetry were recognized by their contemporaries can be seen in Dryden's praise of Waller, 'he first made writing easily an art.' Dryden was praising the lucidity both of subject and treatment, such as were to be found in Denham's *Cooper's Hill.* Four often-quoted lines in that poem became the insignia of the new group:

> *O could I flow like thee, and make thy stream*
> *My great example, as it is my theme.*
> *Though deep, yet clear ; though gentle, yet not dull ;*
> *Strong without rage ; without o'erflowing, full.*

John Dryden (1631-1700), who discovered so much to praise in the new school, was himself one of its chief exponents. Dramatist, critic, translator, Dryden was foremost a poet, and, in poetry, he was primarily a craftsman. This 'man of letters,' whose life was largely controlled by economic exigencies and dependence on the Court, cherished as his first ambition as an artist the making of good verses. He has been widely read and admired, but the English have not taken him to their heart as they have done many a lesser man. Little is known of his biography, and his own verse is impersonal; 'unique vision' he lacked, and his artistry has never had its full recognition. He selected contemporary themes and fashioned them into poetry. In the *Annus Mirabilis* (1667), he wrote of the Dutch War and the Fire of London. In *Absalom and Achitophel* (1681), he transferred the politics of Shaftesbury's intrigues, and Monmouth's disloyalty, into the best of his satires. His *Religio Laici* and *The Hind and the Panther*, in which he writes verses out of contemporary religious speculation, are of less interest today, but one can still admire Dryden's ingenuity in making the beast fable serve his argument in the second poem. As a translator, he rendered Vergil, Juvenal, Ovid, and Chaucer, and the best of his prose is the preface to the *Fables* of 1700, in which, in the year of his death, he introduced some of his translations to the public with a confiding and 'undressed' prose.

The career of Alexander Pope (1688-1744), in many ways Dryden's successor, has been more hotly and more frequently debated than any other in English literature. As often, some confuse the man and the poet. He was puny, ill-made, venomous, unjust, splenetic, and his enemies have found occasion to emphasize each item in the inventory of defects. As an artist, he studied perfection, with a rare singleness of purpose, and he is the nearest approach to a classical poet in our language. It is true that his vision had limitations: the ardours and endurances of romantic poetry he avoided, nor had he the sense of dedication and high purpose of Milton or Wordsworth. In the *Essay on Man* he expressed a philosophy in verse, but rather as moral precepts than as a vision. Superficially his teaching may seem optimistic, but beneath the surface can be seen the alert mind, perceiving the pride of man, his high-vaunting ambitions and, in contrast, the inadequacy of his faculties. If Pope ever forgot that inner vision, he had his friend Swift, close at hand, to remind him.

Thus it was as a satirist that Pope was most effective. At his best, in *The Rape of the Lock*, he was able to mock at the whole of the fashionable society of the eighteenth century, while showing that he had some passionate attachment to its elegance. *The Dunciad*, in which he abused dullness in general, and the contemporary dunces in particular, is more ephemeral until one approaches the magnificent conclusion on Chaos, undoubtedly the most profound passage in Pope's work. The modern reader will find more enjoyment in some of the shorter pieces, particularly *The Epistle to Dr. Arbuthnot*, with the satiric portrait of Sporus, or Lord Hervey, which seem composed in a verbal vitriol, and the quiet but deadly attack on Addison.

Not all Pope's work is satiric. He began with nature poems of an elegant kind, the *Pastorals* and *Windsor Forest*, and the great labour of his middle age was his translation of Homer. This work has often been abused, but, from its own day to this, it has been one of the most widely-read volumes of verse in the language. Homer it may not be, but it is a poem, and one which has given a genuine enjoyment. The charge brought against Pope's translation is largely concerned with the floridness of its diction, and it must be admitted that while in satire he writes with grim economy and with deadly precision, in description and in sentiment he allows the words to weave themselves into elegant and decorative patterns. This mars some of the effect of two poems, *Eloisa to Abelard* and the *Elegy to the Memory of an Unfortunate Lady*, where the gentler and more romantic sides of his nature struggled for expression.

The text-books sometimes speak of the age which followed Pope as if it were dominated by his example. Nothing could be less true. He had only two genuine followers, Samuel Johnson and Oliver Goldsmith, and they both differ from him widely. Johnson devoted only a minute part of his time to verse, but his two satires, *London* (1738), and *The Vanity o, Human Wishes* (1749), both based on Juvenal, show what his powerful mind, his grave moral outlook, and his incisive phrasing could achieve. The graces of Pope are absent, the mockeries, and the stifled gaiety of Pope's humour, but in their place there is a heavier tread, regular and resounding.

Goldsmith, in *The Traveller* (1764) and *The Deserted Village* (1770), depicted the social and economic evils of his time in both England and Ireland. He has a wider understanding of contemporary problems than Pope, but that, of course, does not make him necessarily a better poet. The couplet form for his verse he had adapted from Pope, but he wrote in an easier, more Chaucerian manner, and a mellow sentiment accompanies his expression, so ample, that it sometimes overlays his thought. If Goldsmith had only had a more consistent capacity for taking pains he would have been one of the greatest figures in our literature.

If Pope keeps the reader's attention fixed on society, there was growing up in the eighteenth century an interest in nature for its own sake. Nature had always been a theme in English poetry, from Anglo-Saxon times to Shakespeare and Milton, but in the eighteenth century it becomes an independent theme. Such an interest appears in James Thomson's (1700-48) *The Seasons*, which began publication in 1726. The poem was immediately popular, and though it circulated among the wits, it also had an audience among ordinary people to whom Pope's elegant satires never penetrated. Thomson was too diffuse to be a great artist. His poem is like a schoolboy's essay, padded into the requisite size. Yet for over a century he was one of the most widely-read poets in England. His sympathy with ordinary life, and for poverty, combined with his generous sentiment made him acceptable to many who could not tolerate the hard brilliance of Pope. Also his treatment of nature was original, even if ponderous, and it was a theme growing in popularity.

What this increased interest in nature signified is difficult to record. Part of it was a delight in 'prospects,' in scenes such as a painter might use. Now that roads were improving, gentlemen and ladies could look out from their carriages on the views, and many of them they found good. Some even constructed 'views' on their own estates and parklands. The delight was often not for the pretty and regular design, but for the more wild and rugged aspects of nature. It was as if the human mind were in revolt against the increasing rationalism of the century. Much of this interest was linked with a generous sentiment towards humanity, and towards movements such as Methodism, which drew attention to the great gulf between the wealthy and elegant society of the century and the condition of those who lived in abject poverty. William Cowper (1731-1800) gathers up many of these contemporary interests into his work. He is most widely known for *John Gilpin*, a good jest, but actually the jest of a mind, fretful and tormented, fighting in secret for its sanity. Swift had known that one way of keeping the mind sane when it is assailed by mental disease, is to have an intense interest in details. Such Cowper had, and it makes his *Letters* among the most delightful in the language. Some similar interest helped him to the composition of his most successful poem, *The Task* (1785), where he moves freely amid rural scenes and describes them in a manner less heavy and pretentious than that of Thomson. The composition of *The Task* belongs to his later and happier period, and he had come to that comparative serenity by a difficult road. John Newton, the *enfant terrible* of Methodism, had tormented him, though under his influence and that of his friends the Unwins, he composed the *Olney Hymns*, which include 'There is a fountain fill'd with blood,' and 'God moves in a mysterious way.' Behind all of Cowper's varied moods there lingers the dread that reason might one day retreat, and this led to the most poignant of his poems, *The Castaway*, where, more clearly than in any other poem in English, he shows the fear of approaching insanity.

Morbidity, which threatened Cowper, seemed to hover near a number of creative minds in the eighteenth century. It was as if the sensitive mind in that robust age was driven in upon itself into self-laceration and anguish. Some of this melancholy may have been a fashion, a delight in ruins, spectres, and midnight walks among the tombs, but it was real enough to colour the whole life of Thomas Gray (1716-71), the author of the *Elegy Written in a Country Churchyard*. Gray as a young man had seen the gay and elegant life of Europe in the company of Horace Walpole, but his long years were spent in the enervating life of an eighteenth-century don in Cambridge. Some sadness of spirit within him paralysed action, and made creative work almost impossible. He was among the most learned men in Europe in his day, but his poems are a thin sheaf, a few odes and the *Elegy*. He brought into his poems new interests, medieval in *The Bard*, and Scandinavian in *The Descent of Odin*, but with the whole of the classical and medieval world within his grasp it is sad that some melancholy or inertia held him from composition. A taste for Gray's odes is a cultivated one: the reader must delight in ornate words, often chosen for the memory of their employment by earlier writers. Of the *Elegy* successive generations of Englishmen have already given their judgment, and this can be summarized in Dr Johnson's memorable words: 'The "Churchyard" abounds with images which find a mirror in every mind and with sentiments to which every bosom must return an echo. Had Gray written often thus it had been vain to blame and useless to praise him.'

Gray's depression is genial and controlled compared with that of his contemporary, William Collins (1721-59), whose brief life was marked by penury and bouts of insanity. Collins was not unaware of the life of this time, as poems such as *How Sleep the Brave* show. But the most distinctive side of his mind lived in shadows where the shapes of magic could form themselves. This is found most openly in his *Ode on the Popular Superstitions of the Highlands of Scotland*, but it is present in the ode to *Evening*, and in *A Song from Shakespeare's Cymbeline*. Not always did he write so simply as in this last poem, for he delighted in hard and elaborate words. When he reached simplicity and retained his singing quality he has a rare beauty, which has nothing to parallel it in the century.

The untidy and largely disreputable life of Christopher Smart (1722-71) culminated not merely in morbidity but in the madhouse-cell. There he composed the *Song to David*, written, so the legend runs, 'partly with charcoal on the walls, or indented with a key on the panels of his cell.' The 'Song' has had its extravagant supporters, such as Rossetti and Browning. Even the most sober judgment cannot miss the spiritual vision and the singing quality, rather like a clanging of bells, or the sound of trumpets.

It may have been only an accident that a number of poets in the eighteenth century were afflicted by morbidity and insanity. Yet it would not be unjust to infer that the movement of rationalism, and the bouyant materialism of the time, drove the artist in upon himself. One poet rose against all the pressure of this material world, and though men might call him insane, it was an exulting insanity, the divine frenzy of vision and prophecy. William Blake's (1757-1827) work stands alone in our literature, for no one saw life quite in the same way as he did. If he is to be believed, he actually saw the angels and strange figures which his pictures portray. They sat beside him in the garden, or in the trees, gathering around him as naturally as a group of friends. These visions loosened him from the material world, in which so much of the eighteenth century was stuck fast as in a slough of mental despond. He liberated the human soul from its slavery to matter, and in his more energetic moments saw a life beyond good and evil, a white, burning image of pure energy. Repression he regarded as evil, though freedom from repression he interpreted not psychologically, as is the contemporary manner, but mystically. Much of his thought seems to have sprung fully formed out of his own intuitions, though his reading was wider than is often imagined, and the influence of some mystics, particularly of Swedenborg, is strong upon his work.

As a prophet, and a liberator of the human spirit, Blake is of first importance, but as an artist he is limited by his arbitrary methods, and by an absence of discipline. To disregard tradition completely is the most dangerous course any artist can pursue. Whatever has been gained by our predecessors has been hardly won, and the mental anarchy, which lays it in ruins in order to build the new Jerusalem in its place, smacks of the sin which Lucifer shared with little Bethel. In his later *Prophetic Books*, Blake is in this danger. He uses a symbolism of his own invention, a secret language, bewildering to the reader, and destructive of the unity of his poems as works of art. It is true that, with the aid of commentators, a meaning can be extracted. In breaking the chains which have imprisoned humanity, Blake is in danger of breaking all that humanity has achieved. As a poet Blake is at his best in his simplest poems, in the early *Songs of Innocence and Experience*, where wisdom speaks with the voice of a child. Here and in some later poems such as *The Everlasting Gospel* he wrote with those fragrant intuitions which awaken the human mind to its own best and most innocent vision of itself.

Almost contemporary with Blake is Robert Burns (1759-96). So much that is false has been written about Burns, particularly in his own country, in moments of induced exuberance, that the truth is worth recording. The best of his work appears in the satires written in the *Kilmarnock* edition of 1786. This volume opened for him the doors of fashionable society in Edinburgh where, for a season, as the untutored ploughman poet, he was a lionized curiosity. No journey was ever more fateful to a poet, no people more unwittingly unkind to genius. His moral nature, always susceptible, particularly to amorous and alcoholic adventures, suffered, and farming had lost some of its attractions after the elegances of the capital. Those who found him a post as a 'gauger' in the Excise placed him in an unfortunate proximity to the strong drink which he could never resist.

His reputation as 'untutored,' which he himself helped to

create, is false, for he had read widely both in earlier Scottish poetry and in Pope, Thomson, Gray, and Shakespeare. When he wrote in English, he wrote as a cultivated English poet would write, and his Scottish poems are not naive dialect pieces, but clever manipulations of language varying from Ayrshire to standard English. Nor was he, as sometimes represented, a child of the French Revolution. He was a 'Pittite up to a point,' and a strong navy man, whose best work was written before the French Revolution. He is rightly judged not against the wide expanse of European politics but against his own narrow Scottish background. He revolted against the sanctimonious hypocrisy of the religious, and against the social barriers that divided man from man. This equalitarian philosophy he discovered, not in the text-books of political theory, but from his own observation, and he expresses it admirably, even recklessly, in the greatest of all his poems, *The Jolly Beggars*. After his journey to Edinburgh he composed only one poem, *Tam o'Shanter*, which can match these early pieces. The rest were mainly sentimental songs and lyrics, of the type of *John Anderson my Jo*. It is of interest that both his best poems concern taverns. To the tavern he was attracted for reasons which were obvious, and beyond that, they alone were equalitarian centres in his age, more so than the Church, and certainly more so than any secular institution.

The forms of poetry were changing at the close of the eighteenth century, but this did not deter George Crabbe (1754-1832) from returning to the couplet as Pope and Johnson had used it. So successful was his work that he had a steady following of readers even in the age of Byron. Those who have not read his poems always consider him a dull writer. His themes, it is true, were the grim, realistic incidents of rural life, seen without romantic illusion. But his sincerity in recording life as it was, and his eye for detail, have given *The Village* (1783), *The Parish Register* (1807,) and *Tales in Verse* (1812) an attraction for anyone who may submit himself to it. Some have thought it easy to write like Crabbe, as unfortunately sometimes did Crabbe himself, and this has led to the banalities which the satirists have attacked. At his best, he was a realist in verse, and that is not a mean achievement.

If Crabbe shows that the older manner in poetry still had a fresh life, Thomas Chatterton (1752-70) in his imitations of medieval poetry showed that awakening of wonder which led to romantic poetry. Chatterton's story has passed into legend, but whether the boy who committed suicide at eighteen would have developed into a great genius must remain unknown. He had an arrogant nature, and wit, and had he lived he might have produced verse very different from the sham medieval pieces with which he tried to deceive the learned world of his day.

CHAPTER FOUR

THE ROMANTIC POETS

THE first thirty years of the nineteenth century are marked by a cluster of poets whose work has been as much discussed as that of any group of writers in our language. 'Romantic revival' is the label that has been attached to them by the text-books, though they themselves might not have understood what it meant. The label is only an attempt to show how their work differed from that of their predecessors. They all had a deep interest in nature, not as a centre of beautiful scenes but as an informing and spiritual influence on life. It was as if, frightened by the coming of industrialism and the nightmare towns of industry, they were turning to nature for protection. Or as if, with the declining strength of traditional religious belief, men were making a religion from the spirituality of their own experiences.

They all valued their own experiences to a degree which it is difficult to parallel in earlier poets. Spenser, Milton, and Pope make verse out of legend or knowledge which is common to humanity. The romantic poets look into themselves, seeking in their own lives for strange sensations. With Wordsworth, such sensations have a moral value, and are often associated with simple and human objects. With Byron, they arise from the exotic pursuit of some mood, or adventure, which man has seldom known before. With Coleridge, they lead to the dream territories of Xanadu. In the poetry of all of them, there is a sense of wonder, of life seen with new sensibilities and fresh vision. This strangeness of the individual experience leads each of the romantics to a spiritual loneliness. They are keenly aware of their social obligations, but the burden of an exceptional vision of life drives them into being almost fugitives from their fellow-men. This sense, present in them all, can be found most strongly in Shelley, who seems ever more content amid the dead leaves, the moon-lit waters and the ghosts, than in the places where men inhabit. The romantic poets lead the reader to the strange places of human experience, but seldom welcome him in the language of ordinary conversation, or even with the currency of normality.

William Wordsworth (1770-1850), is at once the oldest, the greatest, and the most long-lived of the group. He died in 1850, but poetry died in him in about 1815, only to return fitfully, almost painfully. As a young man he had high hopes for humanity: he had been nurtured in the Lake District, where everything had led him to think well of man. The teaching of Rousseau and his own experience convinced him that man was naturally good. In the French Revolution he saw a great movement for human freedom, welcoming it as many welcomed in our own days the Union of Soviet Republics. Wordsworth himself confesses that the greatest moral shock of his life came when England declared war on the young French Republic. In the years which followed he had to endure an agony of spiritual disillusionment. He saw that the France of the young Bonaparte was following, not the vision of the liberties of man, but the path of Charlemagne. Partly under Burke's influence, he came to regard England as the protector of freedom against this new imperialism. For the best twenty-five years of Wordsworth's life England was at war, and when peace came it found him a man from whom the uniqueness of his earliest experience had passed. Many of his critics see him as a bitter reactionary, and there is an element of justice in the picture, though it is far from the whole truth. He followed his beliefs honestly to the end, and if he distrusted reform, one of his reasons lay in the fear that the England he loved, particularly rural England, would be destroyed by the hand of the rising industrialists.

The whole of his early life had been a dedication to poetry, and from his childhood he had stored his mind with the experiences in nature which later he was to recall in his verse. This period of intense living culminated in his presence in France during the early stages of the Revolution. All that his nature felt from the excitement of public events was accentuated by his love for 'Annette' Vallon. The biographers seem to have given a shout of exultation on discovering that 'Annette' became the mother of a Wordsworthian daughter, and that he left her to return to England. In the years that followed, under the influence of his sister Dorothy, he recovered a spiritual vision, and a unique poetic way of recording it.

The most memorable account of his own mind in those years Wordsworth has written in his autobiographical poem, *The Prelude*, which was not published until 1850. This is possibly the greatest poem of the modern period in English, the spiritual record of a single mind, honestly recording its own intimate experiences, and endowed with a rare capacity for making the record intelligible. There can be few poems to which the modern reader, harassed by personal distress, or troubled by the movement of world events, can return with such certainty of reward. It would have been well for Wordsworth's reputation if *The Prelude* could have been published immediately on its completion.

In his own lifetime Wordsworth was first known through the *Lyrical Ballads* (1798), in which S. T. Coleridge collaborated with *The Ancient Mariner*. The volume was an experiment, for Wordsworth was attempting to make verse out of the incidents of simple rustic life, in a language that was a selection from the phrases of ordinary speech. Coleridge in his poem was endeavouring to employ poetry to give credibility to the miraculous. Wordsworth's experimental pieces are only half-successful, but in *Michael* he showed how tragic dignity could be given to the story of a shepherd and his son. In *Tintern Abbey*, where he returned to his own experience, he showed, as in *The Prelude*, how a unique experience could be brought within the reader's understanding by bold and imaginative language. After the *Lyrical Ballads*, Wordsworth held less closely to poetic theory. He used the sonnet, as Milton had done, to arouse England to a sense of her responsibility in international affairs, and to express poignant moments in his own experience. In the 'Immortality' Ode, he recorded a mystical intuition of a life before birth, which dies out in this material world, but which can be recovered in a few fortunate moments in the presence of nature. In the *Character of the Happy Warrior*, the death of his brother, Captain Wordsworth, and of Nelson, led him to a noble summary of the life of action. In the *Ode to Duty* he composed in a mood of more classical severity than was customary with him. He describes the more sober moral faith of his middle years, and the same new-found austerity is present in *Laodamia*, one of his rare classical poems. Probably few poets, Shakespeare alone apart, can give more to the reader in the twentieth century than Wordsworth. It may be that his vision of nature was an illusion, but in recording it he pursued many experiences into the secret corners of man's nature, so that few sensitive minds will fail to discover in his poems something that answers to their own intuitions. But his appeal is to the mature mind, and it can only be regretted that his work has so often been forced on unwilling adolescents, who may thus have been taught only to execrate a great name.

Wordsworth's most intimate friend was S. T. Coleridge (1772-1834), and their influence on one another was most productive. Wordsworth had a profoundly moral nature, capable of deep feeling, but controlled by a stubborn Northern austerity. He had also great endurance, and the tasks which he undertook he achieved. Coleridge, on the other hand, saw all knowledge as his province, but it was a province which he never conquered. He 'spawned plans like a herring,' but they were almost all left unfinished. The biographers have treated him with scant justice, assigning his weakness solely to an indulgence in opium. It is true that he was an opium addict, but he took the drug first to relieve the pain of illness, and ill-health pursued him throughout his life. He is not, it must be admitted, a character who easily attracts sympathy, for he indulged in the meanest of the emotions, that of self-pity. To his friends, and to his obtuse wife, he acted with a scant regard for responsibility, yet all who met him fell under the charm of his personality, and the brilliance of his conversation. Further, though he often found the labours of composition repellant, he studied ceaselessly, ever breaking into some new mental investigation.

Though he occupied much of his time with poetry, it is not as a poet alone that he should be remembered but as a critic and a philosopher. In a period when science, religion, and politics were at variance he aimed at bringing them into unity. His attempt is puzzling and inadequate, but it anticipates a modern need, still unsolved. In his literary criticism, particularly in *Biographia Literaria*, he has anticipated the modern philosophical and psychological criticism of the arts. All this should be remembered when the attempt is made, as so often, to judge Coleridge solely from three poems, *The Ancient Mariner*, *Kubla Khan*, and *Christabel*, composed during the period of his closest association with Wordsworth.

From the admirable poem written to Wordsworth after reading *The Prelude*, it is clear that Wordsworth wrote the poetry which Coleridge most admired. He would have liked to have been himself such a poet, gathering the meaning of life as he saw it. A poet cannot write the poetry he wants to write but only the poetry that is within him. Within Coleridge there was a strange territory of memory and dream, of strange birds, phantom ships, Arctic seas, caverns, the sounds of unearthly instruments and of haunted figures, flitting across a scene where magic reigned in a world beyond the control of reason. Some have sought for a moral in *The Ancient Mariner*, and for such as must have these props, Coleridge attached a lesson at the end of his narrative, but the poem itself is like some Arabian tale, where all moves in a weird and unexpected sequence. *Kubla Khan*, though sometimes judged as a fragment, is best considered as a complete poem, and almost as a definition of Coleridge's poetry; the song of an Abyssinian maid erected at the call of a magician. These poems are far removed from the gravity and 'high seriousness' of Spenser, Milton, or Wordsworth. In them the poet is no longer the arbitrator of life, but the controller of a dream-territory, called out of the sub-conscious. Much modern poetry has followed Coleridge in this manner, removing verse from its older and more normal purposes. The strange thing is that Coleridge should have given this lead, for it is one of which Coleridge as critic would have little approved.

Though all their work is often grouped as 'romantic,' Wordsworth and Coleridge had little in common with their popular contemporaries, Sir Walter Scott (1771-1832), and Lord Byron (1788-1824). Scott, in a series of poems, beginning with *The Lay of the Last Minstrel* (1805), was continuing the interest in medieval ballad and romance which had been popular in the eighteenth century. This interest was with him a genuine one, and had originated in his antiquarian study. After his 'raids' into the Highlands he had prepared a collection of ballads and romances entitled *The Minstrelsy of the Scottish Border* (1802-3). From collection he was led to invention and a series of poems followed which included *Marmion* (1808), and *The Lady of the Lake* (1810). After the success of *Waverley* in 1814 his main energies were devoted to prose fiction, but he continued writing verse romances till 1817. In substance and range they cannot compare with the novels, but they use all the romantic resources of chivalry, warfare, pathos, sentiment, and the glamour of an imagined past. They have had a certain survival value and they are better than most critics, and even the author himself in his modest moments of critical comment, considered them to be.

Lord Byron has been over-discussed as a man and underestimated as a poet. Even in his boyhood days at Harrow he had the desire to write, though his first volume, *Hours of Idleness*, is a sorry collection of maudlin lyrics. When this was abused he replied with a wholesale attack on critics and poets alike, *English Bards and Scotch Reviewers* (1809). The poem was unwise, unjust, and impertinent, but it had spirit and a flair for satire. Apart from his verse Byron had already a reputation as a madcap and romantically sinister personality. The impecunious schoolboy at Harrow with the lame foot, had grown into the English 'milord,' proud, contemptuous, lionized, the Napoleon of the London drawing-rooms. That his mind had a more profound mood can be seen from his speech in the House of Lords against the death-penalty for the Nottingham frame-workers. Had he followed the direction of that speech he might have become a great national leader, in an age when England cried out for leadership. But the romantic within him demanded the exploitation of his sensations, not the dreary and exacting labours of politics.

Already he had travelled widely, and his romances had an added excitement of revealing countries that his audience had never been able to visit for themselves. He gave an air of authenticity to his adventures, with even the suggestion that he had himself indulged in similar exploits. These romances, which began with *The Giaour* (1813), captured the taste of his generation. They made his reputation not in England alone, but throughout Europe from France to Russia. More ambitious was *Childe Harold* (1812-18), in which the autobiographical elements are only thinly disguised. The later cantos of this poem combined comment with description. Landscapes, towns, ruins, are all conjured up before the reader, along with Byron's own racy comment. Everything is arranged ultimately to be the background of his romantic sentiment, his passionate longing for some more magnificent way of life, and his melancholy before the presence of the relics of past magnificence.

Byron's greatness as a poet lies, however, not in these poems, nor in his sombre and self-conscious tragedies such as *Manfred* and *Cain*, but in the satires which begin with *Beppo* (1818), and include *The Vision of Judgment* (1822) and *Don Juan* (1819-24). Unfortunately, the prudery of Victorian critics obscured these poems from the public, and they have never received their due esteem. *Don Juan* is one of the great poems in our language, a performance of rare artistic skill. Humour, sentiment, adventure, and pathos are thrown together with that same disconcerting incongruity as they are to be found in life. The style is a clever imitation of the idiom and phrasing of ordinary conversation, used with great cunning for satiric and comic effects.

Though criticism should concentrate on the poetry one cannot escape Byron, the man, for the man intrudes himself everywhere into the verse. More than any of the English romantics he attached importance to his own personality. He was proud of his name, of his power over those who crossed his path, and half-consciously he determined to live out his life so that it would go easily into legend. He felt, as Swift and Sterne had done, the cruel disparity between what life was and what it might be. This vision led Swift to torment and Sterne into Rabelaisian humour. In Byron the two are combined with an added touch of demoniac egoism, suggesting that even if the rest of the human race is to be so bedevilled he should have been exempted. In his release from the inadequacy of life, he sought new sensibilities and new sensations, and his incest with his half-sister 'Augusta' can be partly explained as an experiment in some *terrain inconnu* of passion. Only his morbidity kept alive before him the existence of a moral world, and his sensations were deeper because of his consciousness of sin in defying it.

His spirit might have flourished better in some society other than with the heavy Georgian aristocracy among whom he grew up. The last episode in Greece showed that he had leadership and courage. In his marriage he appears at his worst, and then, for a short time, he seems to have been insane. The world of sentimentality and self-conscious moral rectitude, in which Lady Byron lived, tormented him. He knew freedom of spirit only in Italy, whether amid the wild female creatures whom he gathered around himself in Venice, or in the gentle ministrations of Countess Guiccioli. The admirable *Letters* and *Journals* show how easily his whole nature flowed in this Italian period, and the result was the three satires through which his name as a poet is best remembered.

If Byron exposes the diablerie of romanticism, P. B. Shelley (1792-1822) shows its idealism. To some critics he is irritating and ineffectual, yet considered more sympathetically he is, with Blake, the nearest example of poet as prophet, and he is a greater poet than Blake, and in his life he suffered more. An unimaginative father forced the routine of Eton upon him as a boy. Later he escaped from Oxford by expulsion, for circulating his views on Atheism to Heads of Colleges and others. From then to the end there is no steady track to his life; he seems hurried from one situation to another by some power beyond his will, though in every new crisis he maintains his integrity. His early, rash marriage to Harriet Westbrook can be blamed upon neither of them. That she suffered is obvious, and so everyone was to suffer who encountered Shelley's ecstatic and uncompromising nature. That he should leave her was inevitable, but to attach to him any responsibility for her suicide would be unjust. His nearest approach to happiness came from the earliest phase of his association with Mary Godwin, and after Harriet's death she became his wife. With her his life was spent mainly on the Continent, in Switzerland and Italy, and there he was killed in 1822 during a storm in the Gulf of Spezzia.

Before he was a poet Shelley was a prophet, and his poetry is largely the medium for his prophetic message. He refused to accept life as it is lived, and tried to persuade others of the absence of any necessity for so doing. If tyranny were removed, and cruelty, and the corruption of man by man through jealousy and the exercise of power, life would be beautiful, and an experience governed by love. This message to humanity he had devised in part from the *Political Justice* of his father-in-law, William Godwin, though much of it came from his own reading of the words of Christ and the teaching of Plato. His most ambitious work as a poet lay in an attempt to transmute his teaching into poetry. His success as a poet lay in the fact that, after such comparative failures as *Queen Mab* and *The Revolt of Islam*, he succeeded ultimately in incorporating his message in *Prometheus Unbound.* In this lyrical drama he takes the tragedy of Aeschylus as a model, with the story of how Prometheus was bound to a rock by Jupiter. He modifies the legend to glorify the spirit that man might have if he would take love as his guiding law and refuse to tolerate any tyranny, even though the name of a god were summoned as the sanction.

The theme of *Prometheus Unbound* is the great one of the moral salvation of man, and the verse has a lyrical quality unsurpassed in modern literature. Yet many readers find Shelley's poetry unsatisfactory. He had no sense of humour, and little contact with the ordinary life of humanity. Neither the Chaucerian nor the Shakespearian quality is there, despite his success as a dramatist in *The Cenci.* Nor is this all, for he lacks the grip upon the solid material world which Milton retained. The images which he employs in his poems are always of insubstantial things—winds, dead leaves, sounds, colours, waters. He seems sometimes more of a disembodied spirit than an ordinary human being. Often in his verses he returns to the image of a boat upon a moonlit sea; or the crescent moon itself, shaped like a boat, burning in the clear Italian night. Some such image dwells in the mind even after his verses have been forgotten: an ethereal form in a boat upon a lake and, in the boat a light burning always. If his verses are less read than once they were, and even if he is remembered by that ode *To the Skylark*, the least characteristic of his poems, he has had some permanent influence on life, for with his translucent spirit he has touched the philosophy of progress until it has become vision, and from vision life may come.

John Keats (1795-1821), the last-born of the romantics, and the first to die, has a story as miraculous as any in English literature. The son of a stable-keeper, he spent the best years of his youth in training to be a doctor, though from the first a devotion to poetry occupied him intensely. With very little help from any formal education, and with none from his family circle, he gathered around himself a world of beauty in which he could believe. Out of dictionaries and reference books he discovered the classical fables and legends. From Spenser and Shakespeare he learned the magic power of words, and from the Elgin Marbles, and the paintings of his friend Haydon, he discovered what statuary and pictorial art could contribute. He was genius self-taught, and the rapidity with which he sprang to mature stature is astounding. His *Letters* are not only a brilliant record of his critical opinions, but show his tormented love for Fanny Brawne, his wide capacity for friendship, and the tragedy of his journey to Italy in a vain endeavour to recover his health. Of mature life he had only a few unembarrassed months between the end of his training as a doctor and the first consumptive attack, but in that brief time he produced work which led such a sober critic as Matthew Arnold to compare him, in some ways at least, with Shakespeare.

He followed his first volume of poems with a long romance entitled *Endymion* (1818), which the critics either neglected or attacked vehemently. The poem is over-exuberant, and entangled, but in individual passages it yields a peculiar quality of beauty, as if Keats, knowing all the effects which the painter and the sculptor cannot achieve, had brought them all into his verses. He showed in 1820 with *Lamia*, *Isabella*, and *The Eve of St. Agnes*, that he could present stories in verse, creating for each an appropriate background rich in colour and detail. In *Lamia* he suggested a philosophy along with the story, in the belief that the knowledge gained by imagination was truer than that derived from argument. This theme he explored in the 'Odes,' with great felicity of expression, and with a skilful balance of narrative and suggestion.

Much in Keats's verse seems to indicate that the life of the sensations, and the contemplation of beauty, are in themselves enough. His two unfinished drafts of a poem on the theme of *Hyperion* suggest that had he lived he might have grown beyond this into a great philosophical poet. The egoism, which his earlier aestheticism seems to imply, appears to be broadening out into a genuine social sense. Whether this development of his range of sympathy would have been paralleled by a similar development as a poet remains unknown. *Hyperion* with its Miltonic portrayal of one race of gods succeeding another, the old, though excellent in its day, being replaced by a new and more magnificent order of beings, suggests that had he lived he might have been a poet who was also a critic of life. It is idle to speculate what a poet may do, but in estimating Keats's achievement in his brief years it may be remembered that he was born in the same year as Carlyle but died sixty years before Carlyle's death.

CHAPTER FIVE

ENGLISH POETRY FROM TENNYSON TO THE PRESENT DAY

THE accident of death makes a break in poetry about the year 1830: Keats died in 1821, Shelley in 1822, Byron in 1824, and Coleridge and Wordsworth were poetically 'dead' by 1830. A new poetry came with Tennyson and Browning, though readers at the time were slow to recognize it. The popular poets in 1830 were still Scott and Byron and others who catered for similar tastes: Samuel Rogers with his *Italy*, Thomas Moore with his Irish lyrics, and with the incredibly popular Eastern romance of *Lalla Rookh*, and Thomas Campbell, who in many ways was a more genuine poet than either of the others. The tradition of Scott and Byron, as it was understood in 1830, was one of poetry made easy. Tennyson and Browning were to restore to poetry something of a higher function, though Tennyson can be charged with sometimes having one eye on the audience and, after he was made Laureate, with having both eyes on the Queen. They both succeeded in retaining a large audience for poetry in an age when the novel had become the popular form of literature.

Tennyson (1809-92) has been so much abused in the generations after his death that it is well to attempt to see his performance with justice. No one has denied him a most perfect control of the sounds of English, an impeccable ear, and a consummate choice and taste in words. Indeed, his early lyrics seem to exist only to weave patterns of words, like tapestries, or to create tunes and verbal rhythms, delicate and faultless. The charge could be made that the words were too good for the meaning which they contained. Compared with any one of his predecessors in the romantic period, he lacked originality and depth, and many of the poems in the volumes of 1830 and 1833 have a certain vacuity. The charge would not be equally just if made against the *Poems* of 1842, for here in studies such as *Ulysses* he combined all his early felicity with a theme symbolizing the romantic conception of the heroic spirit.

Tennyson's genius lay in the lyric and the short poem, *Oenone*, *The Dream of Fair Women*, or *The Palace of Art*, but his ambition called him forth to a longer and more ambitious work. Thus he occupied himself at intervals throughout his career with the *Idylls*, his Arthurian poems, picturesque, romantic, but allegorical and didactic as well. The *Idylls* have many virtues, and to hear again isolated passages is to recall how sensitive was Tennyson's ear, how fastidious his taste. Yet once one remembers Chaucer or Spenser or Donne, the virtues of the *Idylls* seem unimportant. Tennyson has reduced the plan of the Arthurian stories to the necessities of Victorian morality. He has failed to look upon his own age with unabashed, far-seeing eyes. The vision of life itself he has rejected and instead made these faultless verses, melodious, decorative and, judged by the great standards, false, The *Idylls* are ultimately the poems of the Laureate; but *In Memoriam* is the poem of the poet himself, and, since it is so genuinely his, it becomes at the same time the great poem of his age. He records the death of his friend Arthur Hallam and his thoughts on the problems of life and death, his religious anxieties and his hard-won faith in an eternal life. The rather fretful mystic, the child before God, terrified of this Universe, and distrustful of the growing evidence of Science, the infant crying for Divine guidance, such is the poet of *In Memoriam*, and the portrait, if not always attractive, is ever truthful.

Tennyson commanded a very wide audience and his imitators were numerous. It was not unnatural, then, that opposition to his verse should grow, and it has persisted from his life-time to this day. He had made poetry the description of a beautiful and antique world, as if deliberately he were closing his eyes to the ugly industrialism of his own century. Poetry, conceived in this way, would not be an interpretation of life, but a charmed and distant illusion. Often Tennyson himself seems to have been aware of the danger, and *Locksley Hall* and *The Princess* and *Maud* touch upon his own time.

Unfortunately, the mind which he brought to these problems was often dulled, and *Locksley Hall* shows that he could be deluded by the mirage of progress which the material prosperity of the nineteenth century seemed to offer. *In Memoriam* alone goes farther and gives not the voice of the preacher but vision, and the strange anomaly is that while the preacher's voice was commanding and resonant, the voice of the vision was like the voice of a little child.

The moral and religious problems which occupied Tennyson are the main theme of Robert Browning (1812-89). He is better known today for his rescue of Elizabeth Barrett (1806-61) from Wimpole Street than as a poet. Of that event only two things need be said. First, the lady herself was a poet in her own right, as her *Sonnets from the Portuguese* and *Aurora Leigh*, which just misses real greatness, amply show. On the whole her verses are more remarkable for their learning than their poetry. Secondly, Browning in his elopement had, as usual, all the luck. If Elizabeth had only died on that flight to the Continent, Browning would have been the ogre of the piece instead of the romantic hero. This must be remembered, for it may in part explain why he believed so optimistically that everything in life did ultimately turn out well.

In pursuing his study of the human mind, Browning drew upon a wide and unusual reading, which easily baffled the reader by the remoteness of its references. Already in *Sordello* (1840) he had employed a knowledge of medieval Italy with an allusiveness which no reader could hope to follow. He had developed also an independence of style, with an assumption of unusual rhythms, grotesque rhymes, and abrupt, broken phrasing. At its best this gave to his verses a virility, which contrasts pleasantly with the over-melodious movement of much nineteenth-century poetry. That he was a master of verse can be seen from the easy movement of his lyrics, but his special effects, though they gave realism to his poems, were in danger of becoming a mannerism.

The appearance of realism through a medium which was dramatic was what he most attempted to attain. In drama itself he was only moderately successful, though Macready was persuaded to play in *Strafford* in 1837. He was happier in using drama without much thought of practical application to the theatre, as in *Paracelsus* (1835), a brilliant expression of his philosophy, or in *Pippa Passes* (1841), where his ideas are simply but aptly shown through a series of human actions. He was interested not so much in the conflict of a group of characters, as in the fortunes of a single mind, and for this purpose he evolved the 'dramatic monologue'; it was in this form that many of his best-known pieces were composed, *Andrea del Sarto*, *Fra Lippo Lippi*, *Saul*, and *The Bishop orders his Tomb*. Their appearance in a series of volumes, which included *Dramatic Lyrics* (1842), *Men and Women* (1855), and *Dramatis Personae* (1864), gave him in the latter half of the century a reputation second only to that of Tennyson.

He put his method to the greatest test in *The Ring and the Book* (1868-9), where a series of dramatic monologues is woven to make one of the longest poems in the language. Browning had selected a sordid Italian crime, which Carlyle sardonically described as an Old Bailey story that could have been told in five minutes, and he so examined the minds of all that came into contact with it that not only their motives, but the whole of his philosophy of life become apparent. After *The Ring and the Book* his poetry develops in obscurity, though some of these later pieces have a subtle interest quite distinct from anything in the earlier work.

He remains one of the most difficult poets to assess. His poems are crowded with memorable characters, and the whole scene of Renaissance Italy comes to life in his pages. At first he seems to have created a world of living people as Shakespeare had done, but a closer inspection shows that Browning's men and women are not free. They live in a spiritually totalitarian state in which Browning is Chancellor and God is President, always with the proviso that the Chancellor is the President's voice on earth. His own life had been, in the best sense, fortunate, so that he knew little of evil, and yet, theoretically, evil fascinated him. Had he known more of life he might have come to realize evil as fierce and positive corruption in human life, and that realization would have deepened his poetry. He also retained an extraordinary innocence in experience which helps to disqualify him as a dramatic poet.

The poetry of the later nineteenth century is far more varied than is sometimes allowed. If Tennyson's was the voice that most people heard, there were many others quite unlike Tennyson's. Matthew Arnold (1822-88), who gave up to the Board of Education, and the necessities of a regular income, years which might have been devoted to verse, yet produced such poems as *Empedocles on Etna*, *The Forsaken Merman*, *Thyrsis*, *The Scholar Gipsy*, and *Dover Beach*. Arnold, who was a son of Dr. Arnold of Rugby, was over-educated for the well-being of his imagination. He had a messianic complex, and in his prose took upon himself the whole burden of the problems of life. He had, like some others in his age, a restlessness in belief, as if he were perpetually crying over spiritual spilt milk. As a poet he would have been better either as a revolutionary or a vagabond. He was neither, but a gentleman, a scholar, and a civil servant conscious of a strange aching in his heart. Often he wished to write poems that would illustrate his theories about poetry, and such a dull poem as *Merope* or such a coldly efficient narrative as *Sohrab and Rustum* is the result. But when he listened to that aching in his heart, he was able to convey his longings, his sadness, even his frustration, in poems which had a quiet and classical perfection.

Edward Fitzgerald (1809-93) certainly did not share Arnold's conception of duty. He lived an incredibly indolent life, but his taste for literature, and his intelligent criticism of it, were his two most consistent pursuits. In 1859 he published his free version of the work of a Persian poet, Omar Khayyam, as *The Rubaiyat of Omar Khayyam*. At first the little volume was unnoticed, but once attention had been drawn to it, the public never allowed it to fall into neglect, and it has been read and enjoyed by many who have read no other poem. The gentle melancholy of the poem, and the romantic style, were, as has often been pointed out, Fitzgerald's addition to the original. So freely has he handled the medieval Persian poet, so fully has he placed into his lines the sad longing which his century knew so well, that though his work is a translation he must be considered as an artist and a considerable one among the figures of his century.

One of the earliest poets to discover Fitzgerald had been D. G. Rossetti (1828-82), and the attraction was not unnatural. Tennyson, Browning, and Arnold accepted the problem of their age. Rossetti rejected it. This son of an Italian political refugee shut out from his work all the moral, political, and religious interests with which so much Victorian literature is concerned. For him life existed only to supply the images of art. Primarily a painter, he had encouraged a group of young men, including Holman Hunt, Millais, and Ford Madox Brown, to abandon formalism in painting, and, with the example of the primitive Italian painters, to execute their works with independence and truth. In poetry, Rossetti had set before himself similar ideals, though his mind, visionary and symbolical, combatted the realism which his principles suggest. His early poem, *The Blessed Damozel*, best represents the conflicting sides of his mind: the detail is material, the theme mystical, but the ultimate motive sensual. Whatever his theory may dictate, his mind searches out for a world of symbols, winds, dim moon-lit waters, strange, rich colours seen in a half-light, not the material world at all but the breath of space. Such was the atmosphere of the lyrics and ballads in his *Poems* (1870), and *Ballads* and *Sonnets* (1881). Love was the main theme that he pursued with this strange combination of the mystic and the sensual, in a sequence of sonnets entitled *The House of Life*. The vocabulary and phrasing he had devised in part from his reading of the early Italian poets whose verse he translated in *Dante and his Circle*.

Egotistical and in many minor ways dishonest, Rossetti's sombre and intense personality had a magnetism which attracted younger men. Among them was Algernon Charles Swinburne (1837-1909), who, after a troublesome career at Eton and Oxford, and a number of experiments in verse, startled London in 1866 with *Poems and Ballads, First Series*. Victorian poetry had been guarded in its themes, and Swinburne, in deliberate revolt, wrote of a love which was passionate, cruel, often perverted, and sadistic. Instead of the delicate sentiments and adorations, there is frenzy, ruthlessness, and satiety. It was as if a satyr had been let loose in a Victorian drawing-room.

The verse with its heavy alliteration and its swaying rhythms enhanced the effect of the sensual. Much of this knowledge of the darker places of passion came not from his own experience but from his reading, which included Baudelaire, whose death he commemorated prematurely in *Ave atque Vale*. He had also explored the less reputable sections of Lord Houghton's library. In his more restrained verse he was reasserting Keats's plea for the pagan ideal of beauty as it could be discovered in Greek literature. His knowledge here was wide and led to one of the most impregnable of all his lyrics, *Itylus*, and to two lyrical dramas, *Atalanta in Calydon* (1865) and *Erechtheus* (1876).

Swinburne continued busily occupied with poetry, and with the criticism of the Elizabethan drama, for over forty years after the publication of *Poems and Ballads*, but the full, overpowering force of that volume never returned. His career has sometimes been described as that of a tropical bird which displayed for a while its gaudy wings in the damp and foggy air of London, and then, since it did not die, had to be nursed, and carefully housed for the rest of its days. In some of the later volumes, in *Songs before Sunrise* (1871), with its praise of the cause of Italian independence, and in *Tristram of Lyonesse* (1882), with its re-telling of the tale of Tristram and Iseult, a new strength seems to appear. But it is forced, and soon overclouded by a medley of melodious words. His early themes had been exceptional, limited, sexual, and once he had exhausted them, he lost strength. *Dolores*, *Laus Veneris*, and *Faustine*, the poems in which he exploited these early attachments unrestrainedly, were the places where his genius stood revealed, unabashed, even if decadent. A few quieter poems, such as *Itylus* and *The Garden of Proserpine*, accompanied that central mood and gained an expression equally strong. But when later he wrote of wider and more normal subjects, poetry gave way to rhetoric and the words swayed into labyrinthine melodies where sound exceeded sense. In Swinburne's poems the romantic manner of making verse as decorative and melodious as possible had been carried as far as it would go. Poetry if it were to live would soon have to turn and find some other way.

Rossetti attracted one other poet, in most ways as much unlike Swinburne as possible. William Morris (1834-96), bluff, energetic, and outspoken, counted poetry as only one of his many activities. He touched upon the life of his age first as a craftsman, a designer of furniture, wall-papers, fabrics, and later as a social revolutionary and a communist. If Rossetti was one of his teachers, Ruskin was another, and from Ruskin he learned that there was no room for the genuine craftsman in a commercial society and capitalist world that thought only of quick production and large profits. Rossetti wished to make beautiful things in an ugly world. Morris, under Ruskin's discipline, wished to remake the world so that all things that man made might be beautiful. As an influence upon his century the later period of social activity is the more important, but the poetry belongs largely to the early period, before these larger purposes were defined.

His early volume, *The Defence of Guinevere* (1858), shows him following Rossetti into a medieval world, and with Malory and Froissart to guide him, he makes poems which are either human and tense, or dream lyrics, beautiful without weight or substance. In his longest work, *The Earthly Paradise* (1868-70), he goes back to Chaucer's way of using verse for story-telling. He misses Chaucer's humanity, and he has neither his cunning in language nor his vivid power in character. In *The Earthly Paradise*, Morris is still closing his eyes to the world around him; 'poor idle singer of an empty day,' as he describes himself, he is peddling his beautiful wares through an ugly world. With the completion of that poem he came to the period of his life when the more immediate task of reform called to him irresistibly. The penalty which he had to pay was that he had less leisure to pursue his poetical work. Fortunately, it did not cease entirely. His visits to Iceland filled him with an admiration for the Sagas, and *Sigurd the Volsung* (1877), inspired by his Northern reading, is one of his most successful achievements. Along with verse he continued to write prose, *A Dream of John Ball* (1888), and *News from Nowhere* (1891): these stories of the redeemed world of the future have had the widest currency of all his work. To some, the imaginative prose stories of his last period have a value beyond anything in his poetry, and it is true that in such narratives as *The Well at the World's End* (1896) he has conjured up an atmosphere that can be found nowhere else.

Two other poets are connected with Rossetti's name, though their manner of life differed widely from his. His sister Christina Rossetti (1830-94), though she admired her brother, lived a devout and religious life, whose values he would not have understood. Her early fairy poem, *Goblin Market*, shows a rich and coloured imagination, which became subdued later as her religious loyalties increased. In Coventry Patmore (1823-96), on the other hand, the increase of spiritual attachment led to an increase of poetical power. *The Angel in the House* (1854-6), a novel in verse, showing that domestic virtue was a poetical theme, has boldness in using poetry for everyday, realistic effects. The more philosophical portions of the poem already revealed Patmore's mysticism, and in *The Unknown Eros*, a series of odes, he developed this with great boldness in language, and with a capacity for revealing intricate thought in verse. As a Catholic poet he far exceeds in power Francis Thompson (1859-1907), whose ornate poetry has proved more attractive to many readers. Thompson's legend of poverty and distress has added to the appeal, and though his advocates have been over-ambitious, it may be conceded that in *The Hound of Heaven* he has described an experience which all mystics have undergone, in an imagery which a multitude of readers, who are not mystics, seem to have understood.

It would be interesting to know how much nineteenth-century poetry lost because of the dominance of the novel as a literary form. Two novelists at least, George Meredith and Thomas Hardy, began as poets, and continued as poets in the intervals of writing novels. George Meredith (1828-1909) began by writing delightful and easily intelligible lyrics of which the most memorable is *Love in the Valley*. This answers the lyrical mood to be found in some of the early scenes of his novel,

The Ordeal of Richard Feverel. The complex analysis of mood, which is characteristic of the novels, has also a poetical counterpart in *Modern Love* (1862). Behind the novels one is aware of a philosophy, and this gains fuller and more explicit expression in his later poetry than in any of his prose. These philosophical poems, such as *Poems and Lyrics of the Joy of Earth* (1883), in their hard and cramped language, attempted to reconcile morality and the teachings of biology. Meredith showed to his age that 'Earth' offered man no easy way of overcoming his brute nature. Bestiality and sentimentalism were always attempting to curb man in his upward struggle towards the normal life, or as Meredith described it, the life of 'common sense.' The novels suggest Meredith's belief that comedy could show man's weakness, and the poems express that faith more openly. As poems they are difficult, even bewildering, but the ground-work of their thought is solid, and rewarding.

Thomas Hardy (1840-1928) is not a philosophical poet as is Meredith, though a settled belief in the cruelty of life, and in the pathos of men and women who are tormented by it, seems to lurk behind all his work. In his many short lyrics, he shows men and women, caught in the tragic irony of circumstance, inflicting cruelty on one another, or pursued by a malign destiny. The brevity, with which these clear-cut pictures are controlled, is evidence of the individual poetic art which he possessed. In the years when his work as a novelist was over, he composed his epic-drama of the Napoleonic wars, *The Dynasts* (1904-8). The range of the poem, with its Overworld, and its widely extended human scene, is held within Hardy's control as completely as the brief, human incidents of the lyrics. He has created a drama too elaborate for the stage, but one which will arouse many clear and moving scenes in the theatre of the mind for which it was intended.

At a time when the vogue of the long poem was declining, Hardy boldly fashioned his great work. Two poems only of the same period can be put in comparison with it. C. M. Doughty (1843-1926), the explorer, whose prose records of travel, *Arabia Deserta* (1888), influenced T. E. Lawrence, published in 1906 the beginning of his long poem, *The Dawn in Britain*. So different was this from the tradition of poetry at the time that it has seldom had its due. Few of the obvious charms are here, nor the softer graces, but in language robbed of all rhetoric, and with incident firmly, even gauntly, described, he builds up a vision of the early days of our civilization. The only other poem of similar ambition is Robert Bridges' *The Testament of Beauty* (1929), which at the time of the first publication had great popularity. Bridges had been writing verse for over fifty years before he came to define his faith in Reason and Beauty in this philosophical poem, which is written in a free measure that sometimes runs a little too close to the harmonies of prose.

It is always difficult to judge the poetry of one's own age, for it arouses enthusiasm or antipathy more easily than the poetry of the past. The modern period in England has certainly not escaped the atmosphere of controversy. All that can be done here is to outline what poets have attempted and to leave judgment suspended. As the nineteenth century closed, so romanticism ended with it. A group of poets captured its last phase in lyrics which have a melancholy beauty. It was as if these poets knew that the words and symbols which they were using would soon be put away as old-fashioned things. From their lyrics they excluded the problems of morality and philosophy which troubled the Victorians, and in brief, poignant lines they found images for their own moods, their loves, and the moments in experience that had affected them. Oscar Wilde (1856-1900) as a poet, was the least important of these writers, though his work as a dramatist, and the notoriety attaching to his name, have given his verses a certain spurious reputation. Far more effective was Ernest Dowson (1867-1900), who in his short lyrics seems to gather up the oldest symbols of which poetry has been made, and to use them afresh. With a more classical severity, Lionel Johnson (1867-1902), built quiet, ordered lyrics which have a calm and reserved beauty. Removed from these writers by his manner of life, but not unattached to them in mood, was A. E. Housman, Professor of Latin at Cambridge. His *Shropshire Lad* (1896) and his much later *Last Poems* (1922) capture in a language which gives the delusive impression of simplicity a number of poignant, even tragic moods. The ease with which Housman gave new value to much-used words and the tunes which he created, his quick, keen references to nature, and the brevity with which he expressed great emotions, mark him as a poet who, like Gray, might have been with the greatest had he chosen to stretch his talent more fully.

Housman has escaped the severer attacks of criticism, but a group of lyrical poets of the twentieth century, 'the Georgian poets' (George V and not George VI), have been very sharply, perhaps unjustly, attacked. They were said to lack profundity, to play with the life of their time: their interpretation of nature was nature seen at the week-end and they were said to trifle even with their deepest emotions in order to turn out pretty verses. Part of this attack centres on Rupert Brooke, who in 1914 published a group of sonnets in which the patriotism, the call to duty, and the idealism of that strange and tragic year are embodied. Brooke seemed to see war as a purifying experience, and death as heroic. A generation which has seen a hideousness in life such as Brooke could not have foreseen, has turned to condemn him. Read today, Brooke's poetry sometimes misses a dimension, though he is far better than his detractors suggest. Among his companions was Walter de la Mare, who still brings to his verse a magic made up of the thinnest mysticism but used to create moods in words that are distinct and memorable. Alone of the writers of this group he lives on to be appreciated by a younger generation in the twentieth century, both as a poet and a prose writer. In retrospect one of the most satisfactory poets of that time is James Elroy Flecker, who used his knowledge of French and Persian verse to give strange and beautiful rhythms to his lyrics.

Much of the revolt against the Georgians came from a belief that poetry in the modern world must discover a new manner. Even some writers who began with a lyrical and melodious verse came to feel the necessity for some expression closer to the temper of modern life. John Masefield, for instance, moved from his early sea lyrics to write grim and human stories, such as *The Everlasting Mercy* and *The Daffodil Fields*. Masefield was deliberately reintroducing into poetry the 'low' world of Crabbe and the human scenes of Chaucer. The boldness and success of his venture, whatever its short-comings, have not always been acknowledged. Masefield's revolt is one which anyone can easily comprehend: he takes the realistic themes which have been neglected, and employs a diction, often itself deliberately crude, in which to describe them. Other poets in the modern period have expressed their revolt in a more complex way. Early among them was Gerard Manley Hopkins, the Jesuit poet, who died in 1889. His work was not published until 1918, when it attracted attention for its originalty in verse and thought. Hopkins' letters show how deeply he had thought about poetry, and he gives a far pro-founder poetic expression to religious experience than any poet since the seventeenth century. He sought to make a poem as compact and unified as a tune, and words and grammar are subdued to this effect. Through him, many younger writers have found a model for a verse that will represent something of the complexity of modern experience. They have adopted his poetic methods, rather than the faith which he was using his poetry to express. They discovered him a generation after his death in the years that followed the war of 1914-18, when his verse, with fresh and vital expression, seemed to answer the same mood as was satisfied by the war poetry of Wilfrid Owen.

Two writers stand out in contemporary poetry, T. S. Eliot and W. B. Yeats. Eliot both by his verse and his prose has made a revolution in the taste of his generation. His early poems, *Prufrock* (1917), were satiric, sometimes comic, always dramatic and impersonal, with an underlying disparagement of the results of so-called civilization. From his reading of French poetry, of John Donne and of the Jacobean dramatists, he had found an acrid and allusive imagery, which pleased the intellect, while it amused the senses by its unexpected rhythms. In a far more profound work, *The Waste Land* (1922), in a 'heap of broken images,' he gathered up the life of post-war Europe and exposed it. The method may be at first troublesome to the reader, for it relies upon a wide range of reference to other writers. Even when it is not wholly intelligible, it captures the imagination. Eliot in *The Waste Land* showed a civilization that had no belief, only a past. For his own part, he came to find belief a necessity, and in *Murder in the Cathedral* (1935) he wrote a verse drama which is Christian in its values. The poetry is much simpler than in the earlier poems, and the theme is made to touch upon modern life and its dilemma in many ways. *Murder in the Cathedral* may mark the beginning of a new poetic influence, though it is the earlier Eliot that has been admired by younger writers. Meanwhile in *Four Quartets* he continued the exploration of the most philosophical aspects of his verse.

It is fitting that this survey of English poetry should end with W. B. Yeats (1865-1939), for in him two generations of English poetry meet. The earlier verse is melodious, decorative, almost pre-Raphaelite, though ever with the difference that Yeats is an Irishman, conscious of his native background. How well he wrote in that earlier, romantic manner can be seen in the way a lyric such as *The Lake Isle of Innisfree* has survived with something of its original freshness, despite the fact that it has been so often heard. Yeats himself came to realize that poetry had to take a new way if it was to adjust itself to the great changes of his time. Unlike some of his contemporaries he did not turn resentfully on the past, but out of his own need made a verse that was at once austere and beautiful. It can be found in four volumes: *The Wild Swans at Coole*, *Michael Robartes and the Dancer*, *The Tower*, and *The Winding Stair*. He had made out of fables and beliefs the images which could hold beauty together in a world where so much conspired to destroy it. Above all, he could stretch his imagination backwards to Swift, and Spenser, and Chaucer, and remember that the strength of the English poet lay in the long and unbroken tradition which he had inherited.

CHAPTER SIX

ENGLISH DRAMA TO SHAKESPEARE

IT is false to consider the drama merely as a part of literature. For literature is an art dependent upon words, but the drama is a multiple art, using words, scenic effects, music, the gestures of the actors, and the organizing talents of a producer. The place played by words, or the literary element in drama, will vary. In some plays the gestures of the actors are of first importance and the words play a negligible part. Here drama is approaching the ballet, in which the gestures have been stylized and the words have disappeared. In other plays the words seem of first importance, as in some of G. B. Shaw's plays, where one actor speaks, and all the others must learn to sit still and wait. The words used in drama may be either verse or prose, but whichever form is employed the general purpose of the drama must be served. Many writers of verse-drama have believed that a play can be made out of a series of fine-sounding speeches. A. C. Swinburne adhered to this heresy, which arose from a misunderstanding of Shakespeare's practice. Shakespeare knew that the play must come first, and the words, however brilliant, must be serviceable to it.

The dramatist, more than any other artist, is dependent on the human factor, and on machinery. The poet or the novelist can proceed as long as he has pen, ink, and paper, but the dramatist must have players, a stage, and an audience. Some writers have written dramas without a thought of the theatre, but this 'theatre of the mind' must be judged differently from the actual theatre, with its physical and material problems.

The beginnings of the drama in England are obscure. There is evidence that when the Romans were in England they established vast ampitheatres, for the production of plays, but when the Romans departed their theatre departed with them.

The earliest records of acting in the Middle Ages are concerned not with plays but with individual players, jesters, clowns, tumblers, and minstrels. Of these the most important is the 'minstrel,' who is a link between the Anglo-Saxon 'scop,' who sang the long poems of heroes, and the later theatre. Throughout the Middle Ages, in his multi-coloured coat, the minstrel must have been a familiar and welcome figure. He could be found at the King's court, in castles, at tournaments and weddings, or in the market-places, gathering a crowd, and speaking or singing his stories. It is recorded that in the army of William the Conqueror, the minstrel Taillefer died reciting the lay of Roncesvalles. On occasion the minstrel could grow rich under wealthy patronage, and lands and valuable presents were assigned to him. Yet the life of the humbler minstrel was at best a hard one, tramping the roads, exposed to the weather, and relying upon the generosity of such audiences as he could find. Officially, the hand of the Church was against him, and there was little hope for his soul to be saved from damnation. At the same time the Church must have seen how the stories of the minstrels encouraged pilgrims in the more weary stages of their journeys. Some clerics even imitated the methods of the minstrels, and stood in public places mingling words of religious guidance with secular stories. Monks, too, were human after all, and enjoyed the minstrel's stories, and sometimes a defrocked cleric would himself turn minstrel.

If the Church did not look kindly upon the minstrels, and their less reputable companions, it was the Church itself that brought back the drama into England. The Church had condemned the theatre of the Roman Empire, and its spectacles and themes gave every reason for such an attack. Yet the ritual of the Church had itself something dramatic within it, and by the tenth century that ritual extended into the rudiments of a play. During the Easter celebrations, such a biblical incident as the visit of the three women to the Empty Tomb was simply presented by priests, with accompanying words, chanted in Latin. One group of priests, or choir-boys, would represent the Angels guarding the Tomb. Three other priests would approach them. The first group chanted in Latin:

Whom are you looking for in the sepulchre, ye women who follow Christ?

The others would chant in reply:

Jesus of Nazareth, who was crucified, O Heavenly beings.

Then the first group replied again:

He is not here: He has arisen as he said he would do.
Go! Announce it, since he has arisen from the sepulchre.

A similar set of words and actions was devised to present the visit of the shepherds to the infant Christ. How the Church came to countenance these dramatic representations is unknown. They seem a natural development of Church services, and possibly it was hoped that they would counteract the village celebrations of May Day and Harvest time. Though their origin is uncertain, it is clear that these liturgical dramas developed in a way which the Church could not have anticipated.

At first, the liturgical play was merely a part of the Church service, but by the thirteenth century it had grown until every part of the Church was used in an action which converted the whole edifice into one stage, with the audience present amid the actors. Such a liturgical play on the birth of Christ is recorded at Rouen. The three kings enter at the east, north, and south of the Church and proceed until they meet at the altar. They chant words descriptive of their actions and then sing an anthem. A procession forms and moves towards the nave while the choir chants. A star is lit over the altar, and the kings approach it. A dialogue follows, and then the kings sleep, to be awakened by an angel telling them to proceed home another way. The procession re-forms, and the Mass follows. It is difficult to visualize exactly the whole action, but no modern stage, except possibly in Soviet Russia, has made the theatre, the stage, and the audience so intimately one. The producer of today may well return to this early drama to gain a conception of what a new form of drama might be.

Such a spectacle was witnessed by many for the sake of the spectacle alone, and there were signs that the higher ecclesiastical authorities were disquieted. The Church, which had reintroduced the drama, was discovering that the dramatic element was growing stronger than its religious purpose. What happened cannot be traced in an orderly fashion, though the results are clear enough. Between the thirteenth and fourteenth centuries the drama became secularized. The ecclesiastical authorities, when they found that the drama which they had created was an embarrassment, removed it from the church itself to the precincts. There, by a number of changes, it became elaborated and secularized. The words themselves were no longer spoken in Latin, but in English, and instead of the brief liturgical speeches, a longer dramatic script was invented around the biblical narratives. The actors were no longer the clergy, but members of the medieval guilds, with each guild usually responsible for one play. The guilds, as a co-operative effort, prepared for certain Feast Days, notably for the festival of Corpus Christi, a series of biblical plays to be performed at various 'stations' in a town. Each play would be mounted on a platform, fitted with wheels, and so could be drawn from one 'station' to another. These religious plays are often considered by the historian of the theatre as important solely in the history of the drama. Actually they are important in themselves. Here was drama as a genuinely social activity, a co-operative enterprise, maintained by guilds of craftsmen, employing their own members as amateurs.

Records show that this dramatic activity was widespread. The number of plays which has survived is limited, though probably representative. Four main cycles have been preserved, those of Chester, York, 'Towneley' or Wakefield, and Coventry. Of these the York is the most complete: in a series of plays it presents the Bible story from the Creation to the Day of Judgment. The plays in the four surviving cycles vary in dramatic skill, though they all show sincerity and independence, with pathos present at times, as in the play of Abraham's sacrifice of Isaac. They have a frequent intrusion of homely and comic characters, as in the treatment of Noah's wife as a shrew. One writer of these religious, or 'Miracle', plays stood out from all the rest, and he was responsible for five plays in the 'Towneley' or Wakefield cycle. In one of his plays, the *Secunda Pastorum*, depicting the visit of the shepherds to the infant Christ, he shows his independence of the biblical narrative by introducing a sheep-thief named Mak, and his wife, and by giving some realistic discussion on the shepherd's life and its hardships. It is difficult now to recapture the minds of the audiences who saw these plays. The main comic incident in *Secunda Pastorum* shows how Mak and his wife dressed up a stolen sheep as a baby and hid it in a cradle, where finally it is discovered by the other shepherds. Could the dramatist have been unaware of the contrast that this grotesque visit to a cradle would have with the other visit, with which this play concludes, where the same shepherds visit the infant Christ? These religious plays formed a great national tradition, which possibly we have never fully appreciated, and England was duller when Puritanism eradicated these pleasures from the people.

Later than these religious dramas were the 'Morality' plays, in which the characters were abstract vices and virtues. At first sight these seem less lively entertainments than a play of Noah's wife, or a sheep-thieving Mak. Some of the authors of the 'Morality' plays were, however, able to make real and contemporary characters of the vices and virtues. So in a play entitled *Mankynd*, the hero is attacked by three rascals, Nought, Newgyse, and Nowadays, and, though this assault has its moral purport, it is presented on the stage as a comic and realistic attack by a trio of gangsters. The possibilities of the 'Morality' play are best proved in England by the effectiveness and the long-continued success of the late fifteenth-century play of *Everyman*. Death summons Everyman to God; his worldly companions gradually forsake him, until Good Deeds alone is left to accompany him on his last ordeal. Though the characters are abstractions, they have relationships which are human, and though the whole action is controlled by the lesson which is to be taught, the play has a natural development, often a genuine realism, with a pathos direct and sincere.

It is difficult to trace the development of the drama at this period, because so much of the evidence is missing, and the historians, who have presented a connected narrative, have achieved a show of order only at the sacrifice of truth. It is clear that, apart from the 'Morality' plays, there existed short plays named 'Interludes.' These were not popular pieces like the religious plays, nor were they allegorical as were the 'Moralities.' They were mainly pieces to be performed in the houses of the more intelligent Tudor gentry. It is known that Sir Thomas More enjoyed them. One of the best is Henry Medwall's *Fulgens and Lucres*, which was discovered only in recent years. The plot shows Lucres hesitating between a high-born and low-born suitor and finally giving herself to the second. Such a theme, though it has a moral flavour, is independent of allegorical structure or of biblical narrative. Once such a theme has been devised, the dramatist is free to go wherever his talents may lead him. *Fulgens and Lucres* has some interesting scenes outside the story, depicting characters from the audience on the stage, in a manner vaguely reminiscent of Pirandello. No other 'Interlude' is so advanced in its structure. The author, who took the Spanish story of *Celestina* and converted it into *Calisto and Melebea*, lost the raciness of the original in dull moralizing. Many of the 'Interludes' attempted less and achieved more. One of the most simple and amusing is Heywood's *The Play of the Wether* (printed 1533), in which Jupiter tries to please all the contradictory wishes of mankind. In this piece there is less structure in the plot than in *Fulgens and Lucres*, but there is an amusing dialogue; and often the 'Interlude' aims at a connected series of entertaining speeches, supported with a minimum of characters or plot: such is the *Mery play betwene the pardoner and the frere, the curate and neybour Pratte* (about 1520), in which these four worthies compete in telling the biggest lie. *Johan the husbande Tyb his wyfe and syr John the preest* (printed 1533) also has witty dialogue, but it has, in addition, the rudiments of character and plot, a domineering wife, a seducing priest, and a cowed husband.

These, and many other 'Interludes,' gave entertainment, with some instruction, to Tudor gentlemen and ladies. Often the humour was crude, the action clumsy, and the road back towards moralizing and allegory ever open. Development in literature is seldom at an even pace, but sudden and unexpected. It is difficult to realize that these 'Interludes' were written in the century which was to see the production of some of the greatest plays in the national drama. How that change came about has naturally been a matter of speculation. While nothing can explain the genius of Marlowe or Shakespeare, the changes in the form of the drama can be in part explained by the revival of interest in classical drama. This influence has sometimes been discussed as if it were wholly beneficial, but this is far from true. The Renaissance imposed a learned tradition, not always fully assimilated or understood, upon a nascent national drama. Whatever was gained, the resulting drama was less genuinely a popular social activity than the the 'Miracle' plays. Yet the classical example gave dramatists a boldness and elevation of purpose, which the native drama had nowhere achieved. In Kyd, and Marlowe, and Shakespeare, this sense of the high potentiality of the drama contrived to reunite itself with much that was valuable in the older native tradition.

The classical drama gave examples both for comedy and tragedy and as far as England is concerned these models were, with negligible exceptions, Latin. George Gascoigne, on the title-page of his *Jocasta*, affirms that he is rendering from a Greek play by Euripides, though actually he was translating from the Italian. English comedy might well have developed without any Latin intrusion, and what is best in it remains native to the end. Tragedy, on the other hand, could not well have grown out of the 'Miracle' plays and the 'moralities,' and here a new start is made in the sixteenth century with the help of Latin models. The Latin models for comedy were Terence and Plautus and some of their influence can be seen in Nicholas Udall's *Ralph Roister Doister* (about 1553). This is a play on the theme of the boasting character, the *miles gloriosus*, of Latin comedy, and though much of its humour parallels the 'Interludes,' the classical model has helped Udall to build a full-length play, instead of a comic dialogue dependent on a few tenuous situations. How strong is the native element can be seen in *Gammer Gurton's Needle* (about 1550), a play which is a little earlier than *Roister Doister*, and can claim to be the first extant English comedy. The central situation in the play is trivial and farcical, the loss and discovery of a needle, but the dramatist had a gift for dialogue, a knowledge of rustic life, and a distinct power in creating characters which include the farm labourer, Hodge, a firmly drawn, comic figure, natural and life-like.

In tragedy, the problem was more severe, and it is still difficult to realize the strength of genius which allowed Kyd, Marlowe, and Shakespeare to solve it. The main model was Seneca, a philosopher of Nero's time, whose moral discourses were known in antiquity, and who was also the author of a series of 'closet' dramas. He had employed the Greek mythological stories, and much of the outward semblance of Greek drama. But the religious element in the Greek conception he had eliminated, and for the conception of Fate he had substituted the more human motive of revenge. The action, which was usually sanguinary, was conducted by the reports of messengers, and this classical economy allowed room for his long rhetorical speeches, in which his taste for moral discourse could be exploited. It was as if a romantic had re-written classical drama to answer his own mood, and a romantic with a taste for atrocities and for moralizing. Seneca was a dangerous model, and yet his strange combination of interests was not unsuitable to the Elizabethan mind. Here they found in the Latin language what they might presume to be the form and themes of the Greek stage, and all this without the embarrassment of the Greek language, which few of them understood. Their own interest in crime, violence, and atrocity was confirmed fully in this classical authority. The moralizing speeches might at first seem more difficult to assimilate. The 'Morality' plays, and indeed the main tradition of medieval literature, had accustomed them to moral discourse. As for rant and rhetoric, they could enter easily into any contest with their Latin preceptor. The major misfortune was that Seneca was not a dramatist, and the main problem which faced sixteenth-century writers, though they were not always fully aware of it, was to convert these Senecan speeches, and the skeleton of his dramatic structure, and his sanction for violence, into a drama that would stand the test of performance in the theatre.

Seneca's own plays were translated and published between 1559 and 1581. Meanwhile, in 1562 there was acted the first extant tragedy in English, *Gorboduc*, by Thomas Sackville and Thomas Norton. Though Senecan in manner, the play has an English theme, and its main motive, of the dangers that follow an unsettled succession, would be of topical interest in Elizabeth's reign, to an audience of lawyers and courtiers. Yet with its long, heavy, blank verse speeches, and its complete absence of action on the stage, *Gorboduc* could appeal only to a learned audience. The native temperament has shown itself ill-adapted to such a complete elimination of action, and even *Gorboduc* made a concession, by presenting a certain dramatic movement in dumb-show between the acts.

This English desire for a play with a more vigorous action is shown in the early popularity of chronicle or history plays, which are a peculiarly native production. The extant examples are probably not among the earliest of the type. They are mainly remembered because some of them presented an outline plan for Shakespeare in a number of his plays: they include *The Famous Victories of Henry the Fifth* (about 1588); *The Troublesome Raigne of John, King of England* (about 1590); and *King Leir* (c. 1594). These and other chronicle plays have action in plenty, but they are formless. The problem, if drama was to develop, was to combine the vigour of this native tradition with the ambition in style and arrangement of Senecan tragedy.

The solution of this problem was the outstanding achievement of two dramatists, Thomas Kyd (1557-95), and Christopher Marlowe (1564-93). Kyd, who was probably writing a little before Marlowe, gave the theatre, in *The Spanish Tragedy*, the play that it wanted. He accepted as much of the Senecan tragedy as was convenient, and on this basis constructed a well-designed popular tragedy. He discovered how easily blank verse might be converted into a useful theatrical medium. He uses horrors and crimes and the Senecan motive of revenge, but his characters are distinct, his situations theatrically effective, and his play a united design. The central theme in an elaborate plot is the revenge of Hieronimo for the murder of his son Horatio, and the dramatic interpretation of the old man is the most human and skilful portrayal which the English stage had seen up to this time. Kyd was the author of a play on the Hamlet theme, of which no copy is extant, but it is clear from *The Spanish Tragedy* that Shakespeare was deeply indebted to the older dramatist.

Christopher Marlowe was a young Cambridge dramatist of wide reading, whose life was tempestuous and whose death tragic. Apart from his brief career as a dramatist, he seems to have been involved in political intrigue as an agent, or spy, and there is some evidence that his opinions on philosophy and religion were considered dangerous. His most important work is contained in four tragedies, composed between 1587 and 1593: *Tamburlaine the Great*, in two parts; *Dr. Faustus; The Jew of Malta;* and *Edward II*. *Tamburlaine* gives best the quality of Marlowe's imagination. As his hero, he chooses a fourteenth-century Tartar herdsman, whose conquests outrival those of any of the heroes of antiquity. Fantastically ambitious Tamburlaine is also grotesquely cruel. Marlowe delights in these excesses, until sometimes he seems to be satirizing his own manner, and the scene in which Tamburlaine harnesses his chariot with kings of Asia became a stock incident for parody in Elizabethan drama. Marlowe is not content to portray Tamburlaine merely as a master of cruelty and conquest. Tamburlaine's lust for power is given a philosophical sanction: he is the single human personality, alone under the vault of the heavens, challenging men and gods with his strength. No enemy overcomes him, except Death, the same enemy that *Everyman* had to encounter. The difference between Marlowe and the author of that 'Morality' play illuminates the contrast between the medieval and the Renaissance outlook. The author of *Everyman* was conscious of life in the world as a spiritual journey, in which the only hope of success lay in a devout acquiescence in God's will. Marlowe, though he knows Death to be lurking in the shadows, challenges the divine rule, believing that the ecstasy of earthly glory is its own reward, whatever may happen. Such a conception of character, depicted with such grandeur and boldness, was without precedent in English drama, and Marlowe had command of a 'mighty line,' a blank verse which could record every gesture of magnificence. Many of these lines linger in the memory of any audience of the play, though perhaps the most significant may be found where Tamburlaine, seeing himself aspiring as ceaselessly as the restless spheres themselves, finds his only consummate happiness in

> *the ripest fruit of all,*
> *That perfect bliss and sole felicity,*
> *The sweet fruition of an earthly crown.*

In *Tamburlaine* this quest of material glory is unembarrassed by conflicting values of a Christian world. This problem Marlowe faces in *Dr. Faustus*, by employing the German legend of the magician who for the sake of universal knowledge sells his soul to the devil. If *Tamburlaine* shows the will to power in the face of material obstacles, *Dr. Faustus* examines the inner, more introspective, and spiritual consequences of such a quest. The play is not wholly successful. Its opening scenes, in which Faustus barters his soul, are magnificent, and the closing presentation of the final hour of retribution reaches a depth of pathos which Marlowe never equalled. The weakness lies in the middle scenes, some of which are crude, grotesque, and even farcical; so inadequate, indeed, are they that some have doubted Marlowe's authorship. *The Jew of Malta* misses the high poetry of the earlier plays, nor has it their grandeur in the conception of character. It descends to melodrama, while it is so extravagant that Marlowe might well have been satirizing his own earlier work. Barabas, the Jew, has been unjustly treated by the Christians, and in revenge applies a Machiavellian attitude to mankind, which Marlowe interprets as the perpetration of a series of crimes, so wild and incredible that it is difficult to realize that even an Elizabethan audience, with its taste for these delights, could treat them seriously. *Edward*

II is, in comparison, a sober play, far more carefully balanced in its structure than any of Marlowe's other works, and, though it misses the fire and glamour of *Tamburlaine*, it has a more varied interpretation of character. Marlowe has converted a theme of English history from the formlessness of the old chronicle plays into genuine tragedy. The central figure, Edward II himself, instead of being aggressive and overpowering, as are Tamburlaine and Faustus, is sentimental and weak.

Marlowe had given to tragedy the magnificent instrument of his blank verse, which, though suitable for 'brave translunary things,' would be found less serviceable for everyday issues. He had also endowed tragedy with a conception of character, and, in a more general way, with the suggestion of unending possibilities of achievement. To the problem of how to build a plot, and to present an action in a genuinely dramatic manner, his contribution had been less impressive. Though Kyd, as a poet, could not compare with Marlowe, he had shown in the structure of a play a skill which Marlowe did not equal.

While tragedy developed in the hands of Marlowe and Kyd, comedy had also proceeded beyond the rustic humours of *Gammer Gurton's Needle*. The most brilliant intelligence to practise comedy before Shakespeare was John Lyly (1554-1606), who was also the author of the novel, *Euphues*. Lyly looked to the Court for his audience, and his players were child actors. It is difficult to realize that the finely drawn sentiment of his comedies, their delicacy, and their elaborate mythological themes belong to the same age as the loud ranting of Tamburlaine, and the blood-drenched stage of *The Spanish Tragedy*. Yet the final attractiveness of the Elizabethan theatre lay in its power of incorporating all of these, and sometimes within the confines of a single play. A number of Lyly's plays have been preserved: *Campaspe* (1584); *Sapho and Phao* (1584); *Gallathea* (1588); *Endimion* (1588); *Midas* (about 1589); *Mother Bombie*, *Love's Metamorphoses* (both about 1590); and *The Woman in the Moon* (about 1594). All of these plays are in prose, except *The Woman in the Moon*, which is a verse play, and a satire on women. They all use mythological subjects, except *Mother Bombie*, which is a modern comedy. Lyly has seldom had full justice given to his achievement, for he is followed so soon by Shakespeare. His originality and invention are remarkable. He combined the realistic farce, the complexity of Latin comedy, and the allegory of the 'Morality' plays into a new design, suffused with a gentle and dream-like romanticism. With his eye upon the Queen, and his audience of courtiers, he gave his mythologies a contemporary and topical reference.

While Lyly works consistently in one manner, a number of his contemporaries attempt a variety of moods. Robert Greene (1560-92), a man of all the trades in Elizabethan literature, a poet, novelist, and pamphleteer, wooed popular taste in imitations of Marlowe, though so clumsily that his *Alphonsus* and his *Orlando Furioso* read like parodies. He discovered his dramatic identity in his comedies, *Friar Bacon and Friar Bungay* (about 1589), and *James IV* (about 1591). He contrived to make a plot in which characters drawn from different social groups and actions with varying degrees of credibility were drawn into unity by an atmosphere of romance. In *Friar Bacon*, magicians mingle with courtiers and kings, and a Prince of Wales woos Margaret, the dairy maid of Fressingfield, and in *James IV* the kings of England and Scotland live in the same play as Oberon, king of the Fairies. Though the road may be a long one it is leading towards *A Midsummer Night's Dream*. Among the other dramatists of the time George Peele (1558-98) is a figure more difficult to define. His *Arraignment of Paris*, probably his earliest work, is a mythological play acted before the Queen, and designed in every way for a courtly audience. It belongs to Lyly's tradition, and though Peele has less sense of design, and less discrimination, he can offer in compensation his lyrical and decorative talents as a poet. His *David and Bethsabe* is an interesting link with the old religious drama. He begins with a biblical theme, but he develops it for the sake of the narrative itself, and for the opportunities of employing his own fanciful verse. His best-remembered play—and, among others, Milton remembered it in *Comus*—is *The Old Wives' Tale*, where a charming romantic opening is allowed to lead into a dramatic satire.

By the nineties of the sixteenth century the theatre in England was fully established, but complicated conditions governed the activities of the dramatists. In London the situation, stated simply, was that the Court favoured the drama, but the civic authorities, partly from Puritan scruples and partly for social reasons, found it an unmitigated nuisance. Those who produced plays, wishing to perform not only to the Court but to the public, evaded the civic authorities by conducting their performances outside the city walls. At first the plays were performed in inn yards, but already in 1576 a theatre had been constructed in Shoreditch, outside the city boundary. Within the city, the one playhouse in the sixteenth century was Blackfriars, where the child actors performed. The actor had to face many obstacles, for by law his profession was not recognized, and he could be treated as a rogue and a vagabond. As a device to overcome the difficulty the players wore the livery of retainers of some lord, or high official. The privilege kept them free from the law, though it left them economically dependent on the practice of their own art. So in the Elizabethan period the companies of players are known as the Queen's men, the Lord Admiral's men, or the Lord Chamberlain's men, according to the great name that gave them legal status.

The public theatre of the sixteenth century differed in many important ways from the modern theatre. It was open to the sky, and without artificial lighting, so that the plays had to be performed by daylight. The stage was a raised platform, with a recess at the back supported by pillars, and roofed. On the top of this roofed recess was a turret, from which a trumpeter could announce the beginning of a play, and from which a flag would indicate that a play was in progress. There was no curtain, and the main platform could be surrounded on three sides by the audience. A few privileged persons were allowed on the stage itself. Hamlet, in Elizabethan times, did not peer out from his lighted picture-frame stage into a dark auditorium, but stood in the light of day, on the raised platform, and delivered his soliloquies surrounded by his auditors. A consequence of this open intimacy of the platform was that scenery, apart from a few essential properties, was impossible. The poet with his words had to supply the atmosphere in which the play was to live. Elaborate and expensive costumes gave colour to the scene, which was comparatively empty and bare. At the rear of this main stage was a background, with a door at each side, from which actors could enter, and also a curtained recess, in which an action could be 'discovered.' The auditorium was oval-shaped, and the ordinary spectators stood in this space, except for the portion occupied by the raised platform of the stage. Around the theatre were galleries, in which spectators could sit, and one of these galleries passed over the back of the stage. On occasion it could be employed in the action for the upper wall of a castle, or for Juliet's balcony. Part of one of the lower galleries at the side of the stage was occupied by musicians, who so often contributed with their art to the Elizabethan drama. In the seventeenth century the enclosed theatre, on the model of Blackfriars, developed in importance. These 'private' theatres were lit by artificial lighting, and more elaborate stage devices were encouraged within them. In Charles II's reign, mainly under the influence of that great architect, Inigo Jones, courtly masques were popular, in which every emphasis was given to decor and stage machinery. The influence of these courtly entertainments was reflected in the increasing attention to scenic device in the 'private' theatre of the seventeenth century.

CHAPTER SEVEN

ENGLISH DRAMA FROM SHAKESPEARE TO SHERIDAN

To the public theatre of the sixteenth century came William Shakespeare (1564-1616) as actor, playwright, and shareholder in theatrical undertakings. So much has been written about his plays, and so much speculation evolved from the few known facts of his life, that any brief treatment may easily be a rehearsal of common-places. Of his life, it is enough to say that, to any unprejudiced view, it is clear that the Stratford man wrote the plays, and that he had a wider reading and more opportunities for mingling with the great than is sometimes realized. Of his personality, it can be affirmed that he had, in an absolute form, the intuition for gathering every 'unconsidered trifle,' and every weighty matter, that could profit his art, with that concentration which is a necessary attribute of genius. Of his art in its relationship to ideas, it remains clear that, despite the divisions made in his plays by categorizing historians, he held to a consistent outlook. In human conduct, he was everywhere possessed by the conception of loyalty and disloyalty, and their consequences in human life. His mind was fascinated by all types of experience, even the most cruel, corrupt, and the 'low', but a tenderness and pity, and an overwhelming compassion never deserted him. In the exercise of the passions, while often entranced with their delights, and ever curious of their consequences, he contemplated the strange conflict of reason and emotion, and the disorder that arose when reason was obliterated. He allowed his characters a freedom to live their own lives to the uttermost confines of good and evil, but he was ever conscious that they existed in a moral world, functioning under a divine Providence. Though his mind often engaged itself with conduct outside the sanctions of Christianity he himself was a Christian. While this consistency is maintained, his art permits of an inexhaustible variety of mood, and, as he progresses, the vision deepens.

He wrote always for the contemporary theatre, manipulating the Elizabethan stage with great resource and invention. The speeches in the players' scenes in *Hamlet* show that he felt the restrictions of the actor's ability to interpret, and of the audience's intelligence in appreciation; but he faced his contemporary audience, answered its needs, and contrived a drama which the Court could appreciate and the public enjoy, despite the competition of the bear-gardens. He was able to satisfy the desire for dramatic pleasure at a number of different levels of appreciation, sometimes even incorporating them in a single play. *Hamlet* or *Othello* can give pleasure to those whose enjoyment stops short at melodrama, but beyond this there is the subtle presentation of character, and a language unequalled in its sources of suggestion. To satisfy his audience was his primary purpose, but this was not enough, for he had to satisfy himself. It is clear from *Hamlet* and *Lear* that he wrote out the play fully as his own genius directed, knowing that deletion would be imperative when his script reached the theatre. With his skill in theatrical invention, he combined a genius for applying poetic language to drama. In the early comedies it seems, sometimes, that language intoxicated him, but gradually he disciplined words increasingly to dramatic purpose. He had a range of imagery which was more comprehensive than in any other poet, and remains a proof of the universality of his interest. He was not unaware of the power which worked within him. Unfortunately, the conditions of his period did not permit of the regular and authorized publication of his plays. Some of them were published in his lifetime with one play in each volume. These 'Quartos,' as they are called, were sometimes unauthorized and corrupt copies, though the circumstances of the publication of the second 'Quarto' of *Hamlet* shows that he was not indifferent to the fate of his work. After his death, two of his fellow-players gathered his works together in the 'Folio' edition of 1623.

His earliest work was in the plays on English history. He wrote, possibly with collaboration, three plays on the reign of

Henry VI. They were the beginning of his epical treatment of English history, from the reign of Richard II to the reign of Richard III. No other group of his plays illustrates his range so completely. In the earliest historical plays he shows some dependence on contemporary models: *Henry VI, Parts I, II, III*, have much of the episodical method of the older chronicle plays, though with an added firmness in characterization, shown especially in the common people of the Jack Cade scenes. In *Richard II* and *Richard III*, Shakespeare adapts the history play to tragedy, following Marlowe's example. In the two parts of *Henry IV* he has liberated himself from any contemporary example, and evolved a drama which, while presenting history, allows for the comic scenes of Falstaff and his company. In the second part the Falstaff scenes occupy more time than the whole of the political action. A well-defined balance of character, especially between Hotspur and Prince Hal, gives a dramatic design to the historical material, while the human relations of Prince Hal and his father Henry IV bring an intimacy into the larger, public movement of events. Nor is Falstaff a mere comic excrescence, for it might be urged that his philosophy, especially his speech on 'honour,' contrasting with the great movement of events, and the high-sounding rhetoric of Hotspur, renders the play a satire on the machinations of leaders, and on the wars which are their consequence. *Henry V*, with its pageantry of national achievement, is no less original in design, and Shakespeare's skill is seen by his elimination of Falstaff at the very opening, so that he shall not delay with his great bulk the action which is to follow. Throughout the history plays, Shakespeare had Raphael Holinshed's *Chronicles*, and other sources, to give him the record of events, but the interpretation was his own. He presented consistently the conception that only by loyalty could the State survive, and that this virtue must be supremely the attribute of kingship. Without loyalty, out of which order and rule develop, Chaos will raise its ugly head, and once Chaos is come, no one will be safe, not even the father from the hand of his son, or the son from the hand of his father.

In the *Henry IV* plays, through Falstaff, Shakespeare matured his conception of comedy, but he had written comedies before he came to Falstaff. *Love's Labour's Lost*, possibly the earliest, is a miraculous invention in which he gives the semblance of courtly life, and graceful manners. How keenly he studied words can be seen here in his satire on all the contemporary affectations in style and vocabulary. In *The Two Gentlemen of Verona* he made his first experiment in romantic comedy, and, possibly dissatisfied with his attempt, he tried the Plautian play of comic situation in *The Comedy of Errors*, with the assistance of twin brothers and twin servants. The play has ample entertainment, though this derives from a mechanism of mistaken identity rather than from human values, and in *The Taming of the Shrew* he returns to humanity, or half returns, for the wooing of Katharina is comic animalism, which the Elizabethan audience enjoyed without sentimental scruples. All these early experiments combine to give *A Midsummer Night's Dream* its magic. No play in Shakespeare is so original, so ingenious, or so perfectly designed. The romantic element is now played out light-heartedly through the lovers, but romance is gently rebuked by Reason operating through Bottom and his Ass's head. The romantic action is enriched by the fairy element on one side, and by the rustics on the other, while the verse gives that atmosphere which Shakespeare can construct distinctively for each dramatic action.

He did not return to write any play similar to the *Dream*, for in that kind he had reached perfection. The play seems to have deepened his own conception of romantic comedy, and in *Much Ado About Nothing*, *As You Like It*, and *Twelfth Night* he brought to the romantic stories, not only a subtle stagecraft, but excellent and well-devised characters. Of these *As You Like It*, with its light-heartedness played out on a background of very gentle melancholy—Rosalind and Touchstone against Jaques and the Forest of Arden—has been deservedly one of the main favourites of the English stage. In incidentals the play is careless, or perhaps one should write carefree, but there is an admirable control of atmosphere and of the central intention. *Much Ado* showed that the romantic story was always in danger of becoming too serious, though this is saved by the good wit of Benedick and Beatrice, and by the very witlessness of Dogberry. All that the romantic comedy could yield is gathered into the beauty of *Twelfth Night*, where amid the graces of the sentiment and the laughter, Malvolio emerges, one of the most finished characters in all these plays. Romantic comedy existed in its own world, and once it faced the challenge of reality some of its values seemed brittle, even false. Often the characters seem to be struggling towards realism, while their master restrains them, so that they shall dance the pretty paces he has designed. Thus in *The Merchant of Venice* does Shylock step out of that fairy world of Bassanio, and the caskets, and the wooing of Portia, and Jessica, and rise to tragic stature as the tormented Jew.

This fantasy world of romantic comedy would obviously not satisfy Shakespeare's whole nature. He continued to employ its pattern in *All's Well that Ends Well*, and in *Measure for Measure*, where the vision which he had to unburden was too profound for its moonshine delights. The contrast between the story and the vision gives these plays a strange atmosphere, so that they have been named 'the dark comedies.' In them Shakespeare seems for some reason to be clinging to romantic comedy when tragedy was his proper medium.

It may have been the same mood which led him to *Troilus and Cressida*, where he seems contemplating satirically the Grecian world which men had called heroic. His satire exposes the treachery of love, the deceit of honour, and the uselessness of war, and in this play hope is unknown. The great period of Shakespeare's tragedy is to be found in the plays which begin with *Hamlet*, and include *Othello*, *Macbeth*, *King Lear*, *Antony and Cleopatra*, and *Coriolanus*. These were all composed in the first six years of the seventeenth century. It would, however, be false to consider Shakespeare's achievement in tragedy as confined to these great plays. Already in the English history plays he had found a form of tragedy, partly with Marlowe's aid, in *Richard II* and *Richard III*. He had turned from the romantic comedies to fashion the romantic tragedy of *Romeo and Juliet*. In *Julius Caesar* he had combined Roman history with the interpretation of Brutus's tragic character.

Tragedy, then, belongs not exclusively to any single period of his work, but is with him in all stages of his career, except the last. At the same time, in the period of the great tragedies, his vision seems deeper, and his powers in verse, and in dramatic genius, appear at their supreme. The great tragedies share some characteristics. Each portrays some noble figure, caught in a difficult situation, when some weakness, or bias, of his nature is exposed. Upon his action depends not only his own fate, but that of an entire nation. While attention is concentrated on this central action, Shakespeare portrays the whole world in which his hero moves. Each of the plays is so made that it can appeal to different audiences at different levels of intelligence. *Hamlet* is a story of murder, suicide, madness, to those who call for melodrama, but for others it is a more subtle analysis of character, and a play in which verse is used with great sublety.

Hamlet, the earliest of the great tragedies, is the most self-conscious. The Renaissance atmosphere of art, ostentation, learning, and crime, governs a play, in which the central character is himself a Renaissance scholar-prince, clever, melancholic, introspective. Like a character in life itself, Hamlet may not be capable of full interpretation, though it is clear that through him Shakespeare explored the whole problem of action and the reflective mind. In *Othello* he showed that he could compose a much more closely designed play, where the theme is as compact as an argument. Never did his knowledge of the stage show itself more completely, for the much-praised Iago owes his existence only to his master's knowledge of what the stage can make credible. If that fine villain stepped out of the theatre, as so many critics encourage him to do, he would fall into the hands of the veriest Dogberry of a policeman. The verse, which served the action so admirably in *Othello*, reaches a greater height of magnificence in *Macbeth*, though as a tragedy the piece has been overpraised. No actor has made his reputation by playing Macbeth, a part difficult to make interesting, and impossible to make convincing. It may be that the character is too great for the actor, but certainly the full poetic significance of the tragedy does not appear in the theatre.

Lear, the 'epic' of the tragedies, is rugged, primitive, and Wagnerian. It cannot be appreciated if it is thought of in the terms of the modern stage. Once scenery and all the appurtenances of realism have gone, Lear may stand out in the storm scenes as the greatest figure in our literature, but the absence of the graces and variety of *Hamlet*, and the incredible opening, will leave it the most admired, rather than the best loved of these plays. It is a better tragedy for the theorist than for the theatre. *Antony and Cleopatra* stands apart, for in none of the other tragedies has love been given such a part in the plot, or woman such a place amid the *dramatis personae*. Critics have often condemned the play as being too diffuse. How many of these critics have ever seen it acted in its entirety? The two central characters, particularly Cleopatra, are among the best observed and most realistic in Shakespeare. *Coriolanus*, in marked contrast, is a tragedy, political in theme and austere in treatment, with an almost classical economy in its closing scenes. It is a play which required supreme production in the theatre and for this reason is seldom successfully rendered.

What brought the tragic period in Shakespeare to a close no one can tell. Some change of vision, perhaps even a creative exhaustion, led him on to the changed atmosphere of the last romances, *Cymbeline*, *The Winter's Tale* and *The Tempest*. The view most generally accepted by modern critics is that his work for the 'private' theatre at Blackfriars led him to an action, more elaborate in incident, and more dependent on stage effects. In the early scenes of *The Winter's Tale* he can be seen handling again the 'Othello' theme, but the language breaks under the pressure of his vision. Suddenly he rejects it all, and enters into a pastoral world, beautiful and genial, where instead of tragedy there is reconciliation. It can be argued that this last mood was always present, and that it is only part of the Christian teaching of atonement and forgiveness. Even at the close of *Lear* there is an almost mystical recognition of pity and reconciliation. Yet in these last plays all is changed, for the reconciliation is made too easily. Through Lear's world there blew a storm, wild and uncontrollable, but the storm in *The Tempest* answers Prospero's every gesture.

This last play has, however, like *A Midsummer Night's Dream*, a miraculous quality, for it seems compact of originality. The characters are half-allegorical, the theme full of suggestions, the action a unity, and all made beautiful, except for the evil of Caliban, and in him it would seem that Shakespeare, having exhausted humanity in his previous creation, went outside man, and made a monster all of his own devising.

The genius of Shakespeare should not allow the rest of the drama of his age to be obscured. Contemporary with him was Ben Jonson (1573-1637), a combative, powerful personality, in almost every way a contrast to him. Jonson was a classicist, a moralist, and a reformer of the drama. In comedy he turned his back upon romance, and presented the London of his own day with a strenuous effort towards realism, and an attempt to contain the action within the 'unities' of time, place, and theme. Nor was he content that his excellence should escape the attention of his audiences. In prefatory verses he will thunder out the virtues of his play, like some dowager presenting estimable but ungainly daughters. While Shakespeare is showing Belmont and the Forest of Arden, Jonson depicts the rogues of Bartholomew Fair and Thames Side. From his first successful play, *Every Man in his Humour*, he showed a consistency of method, though with much development in skill. His characters were, as he described them, 'humours' characters: one element in their moral nature was displayed throughout the play and exposed for ridicule. The nearest approach to this method in Shakespeare is in Malvolio, but Jonson used this 'static' type of character with great success to emphasize the weakness and the moral diseases of human nature. His gallery of 'humours' is so extensive that he is in a way the Dickens of the seventeenth century, though without Dickens's sense of buoyant high spirits, or his sentimentality. The corruption of the new wealth, which commerce was giving to the middle classes, affected Jonson deeply enough for him to add bitterness to his comedy.

In four plays his original mind, working within its self-prescribed limitations, achieved outstanding success, and they have been seen on the English stage less often than they deserve: *Volpone*, *The Silent Woman*, *The Alchemist*, and *Bartholomew Fair*. Of these, the most perfect in structure and delightful in its treatment is *The Alchemist*, the most brilliant realistic comedy in the whole Elizabethan theatre. *Volpone*, a study of avarice on the heroic scale, has a Rembrandtesque grandeur in colouring, to which none of the other plays attains. *Bartholomew Fair* is the most Dickensian of the plays, a confident picture of Elizabethan 'low' life. *The Silent Woman*, in lighter mood, approaches the comedy of manners which was to delight Restoration audiences. In tragedy, Ben Jonson was less successful. *Sejanus* and *Catiline* can claim the pedantic virtue of being an attempt to write Senecan drama in English: they have the spurious 'correctness' of attempting to keep drama to the detailed truth of history. It is not enough: the verses will not move; as Tennyson said, they were like glue, and the characters will not come to life. In comedy Jonson's genius is found at its best, and his influence was considerable. The Restoration dramatists leaned strongly upon him. It is only to be regretted that from the eighteenth century the idolatry of Shakespeare has deprived Jonson of the place which should be his upon the English stage, though the twentieth century has seen some revivals.

Jonson is at once the clearest personality and the most original of the dramatists of Shakespeare's age. He was also the most learned, unless that claim were challenged by George Chapman (1559-1634), who is more famous for his translation of Homer than for his dramas. There is evidence that Chapman did a number of jobs of all work in the Elizabethan theatre, but his most distinctive achievement was in three historical tragedies: *Bussy D'Ambois*; *The Revenge of Bussy D'Ambois*; and *The Tragedy of Biron*. He chose French history as his background, though mingling it freely with his own invention, and in the Bussy plays his scene is a contemporary one. In Bussy, he drew the proud character on Marlowe's model, allowing him a bold licence in speech and action, as he asserts himself in the French Court. As one reads Chapman's plays one can only wonder that any audience found them intelligible. The speeches which crowd from his pen, are full of elaborate metaphors, phrase tumbling after phrase, until the mind is bewildered by a brilliant but confused riot of words. The reader, who has the leisure to turn over the sentences, dissecting them into orderliness, finds himself in the presence of a philosophical mind, but the audience in the theatre, unless it was far more intelligent than any contemporary audience, must have found itself baffled. Yet Dryden spoke unjustly of Chapman when he described his style as 'a dwarfish thought, dressed up in gigantic words,' for his intellect was powerful.

While the drama of the early seventeenth century has certain common characteristics, it is not difficult to distinguish a number of distinctive types. The element of realism, which Jonson mastered, was pursued by a number of writers. Thomas Dekker (1570-1641) combined it with a genial vein of romantic sentimentality. In *The Shoemaker's Holiday* he gives the happiest pictures of the workmen and apprentices of London, and in Simon Eyre, the shoemaker who became Lord Mayor, he glorifies the workers in whom he delights. Later, in the more profound play of *The Honest Whore*, he added pathos to his sentimentality, and employed his realism in an alert portrayal of character. While Dekker depicted the citizens, Thomas Heywood (1575-1641), notably in *A Woman Killed with Kindness*, adapted tragedy to the sensibilities of the rising middle classes. The values contrast with the heroic standards of Shakespeare's *Othello*; for high tragedy Heywood substitutes sentiment and introspective morality. The citizens were, however, not always presented favourably in the drama. Those who wrote with their eye on the Court watched the manners of the City and the apprentices with a critical eye. Beaumont and Fletcher in *The Knight of the Burning Pestle* used their observation to make a merry game of the credulity of the citizens and of their delight in romantic stories.

John Fletcher (1579-1625) and Francis Beaumont (1584-1616) wrote for some years in happy collaboration. As dramatists they have suffered, because critics will compare their work with Shakespeare's. Three plays show them at their best: the tragi-comedy *Philaster*, and two tragedies, *The Maid's Tragedy* and *A King and No King*. The world they depict is removed from the ordinary world which men know. Upon the background of an artificial courtly life they portray exaggerated passions, often corrupt and unnatural, high-flown sentiments, and honour coded into elaborate formularies. The plots, which carry the burden of their devices, are elaborate, but invented with great ingenuity, and admirably conducted. Their verses, too, have a softness and grace, which are pleasing, and in the scenes of strong emotion there is an undoubted strength. Keep out the Shakespearian comparison and Beaumont and Fletcher appear as dramatists of many virtues. Once the comparison is made, the quality falls out of their world. Their grace becomes lifeless, the verses miss profundity, and the artifice looks as strange as the garments of masquerade seen against the midday sun.

Beaumont and Fletcher had failed to give tragedy the normality which Shakespeare retained. Nor were they alone in thus limiting its range. The first forty years of the seventeenth century produced a number of examples of tragedy conceived in some extravagant and unreal world, or developed with a disregard for the motives of good and evil, or, indeed, in defiance of the moral order of being. The most profound of these tragic writers is John Webster (1575-1625), who is remembered for two plays, *The White Devil* and *The Duchess of Malfy*. Both plays depend on the 'revenge' theme, which was already popular when Shakespeare wrote *Hamlet*, and continued in favour throughout these decades. Webster succeeds in building a world around his plots, but it is the sinister world of Renaissance Italy, where cunning is the equivalent for good, and where intrigue, contrived with the most ingenious devices, is elevated into a fine art. At first sight his plays seem mere melodrama, where horror is exploited, and violence displayed. It is true that he troubles little to construct his plots. He is content to concentrate on certain theatrically effective scenes, and is careless whether the scaffolding holding them together is clumsy or too obviously visible. Yet when these two plays are read, or seen in the theatre, it is soon apparent that they are more than melodrama. Behind this world of theatrical violence, Webster, with a poet's mind, sees life itself as pitiless, cruel, and corrupt, and this elevates his violence into vision. He extends no mercy to his characters, as his treatment of the Duchess of Malfy shows, but sometimes, in a few lyrical lines, he suggests that he is aware of the cruel nature of the universe, and the sadness that existence should be thus. His admiration goes out to the characters who defy the sordidness of life, and risking all the dangers of retribution live beyond good and evil, in magnificence. So the White Devil, in her trial scene, stands out as the greatest figure in his plays: she is an adultress and an accessory to murder, but she has a corrupt nobility, and in a world where all is corrupt that is the equivalent of nobility itself.

Cyril Tourneur (1575-1626) in *The Revenger's Tragedy* and *The Atheist's Tragedy* drew a world more abnormal than that of Webster. In *The Revenger's Tragedy* he depicts a Court governed by lechery and cruelty. So corrupt are his characters that they seem symbols of the vices rather than human figures. These unnatural puppets he moves with the precision of a master of some macabre ballet, and this certainty of theatrical intention gives an intensity to the whole action. Like Webster, he is a poet, and the verse, by its imagery, suggests a world where, beneath the light of the torches, one can see the sinister faces, the monstrous intrigues, the scenes of horror, and the lurking figure of the Revenger.

While Webster and Tourneur can best be remembered for one type of play, there are some dramatists of this period who are versatile in a bewildering way. Many of them worked in collaboration, and it is difficult to assign any exact responsibility for authorship. Such problems occur in considering Thomas Middleton (1570-1627), who wrote comedies, including the uproarious *A Chaste Maid in Cheapside*, and tragedies. Outstanding is *The Changeling*, a play in which he collaborated with William Rowley. This tragedy seems a compound of Shakespeare and Webster: its theme is romantic and its characters evil, but around the central figure of Beatrice, despite the fact that she has instigated a murder, the more human values of Shakespeare are retained. She is forced by her passion to place herself in the power of a vicious and merciless lover,

De Flores, and her horror and loneliness, despite her crime, arouse pity in the audience.

Philip Massinger (1584-1639) shared much of the versatility of Middleton. Yet, so far as the history of the stage is concerned, his foremost success was a comedy, entitled *A New Way to Pay Old Debts*. Here, in Sir Giles Overreach, he portrays a miser, who combines this vice with cruelty and a love of power. Massinger shares Jonson's power of showing human nature as diseased, but in the severity of the satire, Massinger exceeds Jonson. It is almost as if he had taken a terrified glance at the heartlessness of the rising commercial classes, and attempted to shame them into some kindliness of heart by this scarifying picture of their vices.

In the years before the theatres were officially closed by the Puritans in 1642, there was little new development in the drama. Rather it would seem that the old themes were being played again, though with added excesses. Compared with Dekker, or Shakespeare, or Jonson, the drama of those later years is decadent. It insists upon unnatural passions, intricate crimes, and devices of horror. It can be redeemed only when it is handled by a poet, and the remarkable feature of the whole drama of that period is the excellence of the poetry which was at its service. So did John Ford (1586-1639) in *'Tis Pity She's a Whore* and in *The Broken Heart* employ poetry to bring pathos and a tender feeling to plays whose themes dwell amid incest, horrors, and perversities. So did James Shirley (1596-1666), as he touched again many of the types of drama that had preceded him, bring verse to endow them with a brightness which they would not otherwise have possessed.

With the Civil Wars the greatest period in English drama came to a close. Nothing was the same in England after that conflict, and the drama never again had the same brilliance, or the same contact with the whole of the national life. When this drama began with Marlowe, men were near enough to the Middle Ages to be touched by the living terrors of sin and death, and near enough to the Renaissance to feel its magnificence, and the new and perilous adventures which were indicated to the spirit of man. Almost unseen, the powers of commercialism were contaminating that world with new and gross values. If magnificence were to survive, it had to dwell apart, removed from life. It had existed as a wraith in the masques of the Stuart Courts, for Charles I, whatever his weaknesses, had enjoyed the arts. The masque was a dramatic artifice in which poet and stage designer met to make an entertainment with dances, music, and elaborate scenic devices. The court was fortunate that for the words of the masque it could call on poets such as Jonson, Chapman, and Carew, and for the design upon a great architect such as Inigo Jones. The scenic elaboration of the masque had its effect on legitimate drama, as can be seen in Shakespeare's *Tempest*. But in the seventeenth century the vision of the dramatist did not keep pace with the mechanical devices at his disposal. The national spirit in the drama had disintegrated, and though much that is brilliant is to follow the old way could never return.

When Charles II came back with the Restoration of 1660 the theatres were reopened. Actually the break between 1642 and 1660 was not complete, for entertainments of one kind or another had continued. Nor were the older writers forgotten: Jonson's plays reappeared on the Restoration stage; Shakespeare was no less a favourite, though his plays were modernized to meet the fashions of the day. Spiritually the change was profound. The Restoration was not only the period of Charles's Court, but the age of Bunyan, of the Royal Society, and the philosophy of Locke. The drama did not represent the age, for the drama became only an entertainment for the Court, and those that aped its fashions. It answered only to one side of men's needs. Samuel Pepys was a very regular playgoer, and much that Pepys saw upon the stage he practised himself in his more idle and less responsible moments when opportunity arose; but Pepys, the founder of the Navy, could not have discovered in that theatre anything to answer the deeper and more creative part of his nature.

It was in comedy that the Restoration found its peculiar excellence. The comedies of that period were many and varied, but it was in the work of three writers, Etherege, Wycherley, and Congreve, that the one distinctive type, the comedy of manners, was evolved. Sir George Etherege (1635-91) in *The Man of Mode* first discovered the formula. In a comedy absolved from all obligation to portray a moral world, and from which romantic elements were excluded, he gave a witty portrayal of elegant ladies and gentlemen of the day in their conversation and their amorous intrigues.

The more powerful mind of William Wycherley (1640-1716) penetrated deeper into the world which Eltherege had displayed. He presents the same elegant, immoral scene, but he portrays it with mockery and satire. He has a more virile and boisterous nature than any other writer of the period, and a greater restlessness. In the drama he has studied Jonson, and he knows Molière's plays, and borrows from them without attempting to adapt his own violent nature to the graces of Molière's world. With four plays he has held a permanent place on the English stage: in *Love in a Wood* (1671) and *The Gentleman Dancing-master* (1673) he is still experimenting, but *The Country Wife* (1675) and *The Plain Dealer* (1676) show him fully in possession of his powers. He had studied his world closely, and Jonson's model had taught him to depict character in strong and vivid colours. The intrigue, the gaiety, the foibles, all these he conveyed, though one is conscious amid the laughter of his contempt for society, and possibly for life itself. His satire is not founded on moral scruples, but on his cynical mockery of the human puppets who pursue their pleasures and find them so illusory.

William Congreve (1670-1729), the most elegant of the trio, drew back from the depths which Wycherley had exposed, and returned to the surface gaiety of Etherege. At the same time he conducted his comedies with a brilliance of dialogue which Etherege had never achieved. He had made his reputation suddenly and easily at the age of twenty-five with *The Old Bachelor* (1693). Three comedies followed: *The Double Dealer* (1694); *Love for Love* (1695); and *The Way of the World* (1700). With these he had written one tragedy, *The Mourning Bride* (1697), before, at the age of thirty, he turned his back upon the stage.

His greatness as a dramatist lies in the completeness of his vision. It is the vision of a very shallow world, but he has an exquisite accuracy in depicting its values. The triumph in his world is not of good over evil, but of the elegant over the inelegant, of the witty over the dull, of the graceful over the boorish. Sentiment is never allowed to intrude, nor morality, in an assembly where the right artifice in manners, fashion, and conversation gives the only passage to success. Judged from the standard of morality, as Lord Macaulay was later to judge it, this world is false. These fashionable doors have been closed, to hush any cry from suffering humanity that might disturb the gaiety going on so elegantly within them. But one would not condemn a ballet because it does not arouse the same emotions as *King Lear*, or Mozart because his music is not that of Beethoven. Congreve's greatness as an artist lies largely in his knowledge of what he should exclude so that this brilliant, selfish world might display all its bright colours unimpeded. This he did with admirable success in the spontaneous humour of that adroitly constructed comedy, *Love for Love*. With greater deliberation he achieved a more subtle effect in *The Way of the World*, where in Millamant he made one of the great comic figures of the English stage.

The brilliant indecencies of Restoration comedy did not pass without criticism. Jeremy Collier, in the *Short View of the Immortality and Profaneness of the English Stage*, brought the weight of the Church and middle-class society to bear against the drama, in an elaborate and scholarly indictment. It cannot be said that any immediate moral improvement is apparent, though gradually, in the eighteenth century, middle-class values had an increasing hold on the drama. Before this calamity, Sir John Vanbrugh wrote *The Relapse* (1696), in which it would be difficult to find any concession to Collier, unless it is in the few touches of sentimentality. In 1707 George Farquhar wrote *The Beaux' Stratagem*, which in a way is a link between the manners comedy and the broader world of the eighteenth-century novel. Here instead of the London drawing-rooms are the inn on the coaching road and the country house, and with the gentlemen mingle ostlers and highwaymen.

Nothing in the Restoration drama matches the comedy. The 'heroic drama' of that age is now remembered only in the text-books of literature. In this strange form the motives of love and honour were exaggerated to incredible lengths, and the characters were given grandiose and ranting speeches, which they declaimed in regular heroic couplets. The psychologist may find these plays interesting, for they suggest that an audience, whose life was governed by cynicism, found some relief in this dream-world picture of a fantastic conception of honour. The one notable thing about the heroic drama is that Dryden devoted his great talents to it. Of this kind his best play was his *Aurengzebe* (1675). Much of his prose, which began in 1668 with *An Essay of Dramatic Poesy*, was concerned with the heroic play, and it is to be regretted that such an admirable writer was restrained by such a poor subject. The heroic play was too bizarre a fashion to live long. Dryden in *All for Love*, re-telling the Shakespearian story of Antony and Cleopatra, had given up the rhyming absurdities of the heroic play for a closely presented action in blank verse. With even greater success, Thomas Otway, in 1682, returned to the Elizabethan manner in *Venice Preserved.*

The drama of the eighteenth century does not reach the same high level as the novel. One has to wait late in the century, for Goldsmith and Sheridan, to find writers who make any permanent contribution to the English stage, and even then there is nothing to equal *Tom Jones* or *Tristram Shandy*. Of a number of reasons which might be invented in explanation it is at least certain that the Licensing Act of 1737 restricted freedom of expression by dramatists and drove a number of good men out of the theatre. Henry Fielding had been a dramatist before that date, and without Walpole, and the Licensing Act, his more mature genius might have gone into the theatre instead of the novel. From 1737 to the present day the theatre has been hampered by the restrictions of censorship. Further, it was clear also that the middle-class commercial classes were gaining sufficient ascendancy to impose their obtuse views on the themes that would be acceptable in the theatre. If the century can make no claim to dramatic supremacy, it possesses two names which stand pre-eminent in our acting tradition. The art of the actor is pathetically ephemeral, and he is in danger of being forgotten as soon as the applause has died away after his last exit, but despite this the names of Garrick and Mrs. Siddons have become some permanent part of the English tradition. In the same way in the early nineteenth century Kean as an actor is far greater than any dramatist of the period.

Outstanding in the early decades of the century is John Gay's *The Beggar's Opera* (1728). The permanent appeal of the lyrics of Macheath, the highwayman, of Polly and of the whole of this 'Newgate pastoral,' has remained to the present day, but it had an added piquancy to audiences who could detect within it a satire on Walpole. *The Beggar's Opera* was imitated both by Gay and by others, but it has no parallel. Comedy in the early eighteenth century suffered a sad decline into sentimentalism. The history of sentimentalism is unwritten, yet without it the interpretation of modern England is incomplete. Sentiment may be defined as feeling, and in the eighteenth century, against the background of much crudity and barbarism, there developed both in life and in literature an increase of this power to feel. In religion it can be discovered in movements such as Methodism, in social life in an increasing realization of the hardships, which the majority of mankind had to suffer. Its dangers are obvious, for it leads to emotional indulgence instead of mysticism, and to charity instead of genuine reform. It clouds the reason, substitutes pathos for tragedy, and obscures the harder issues of life in a mist of tenderness. In literature its effects were numerous, and, in comedy, disastrous. An early exponent of sentimentalism was Richard Steele, who had been Addison's collaborator in *The Spectator*. In plays such as *The Tender Husband* (1705), he extolled the domestic virtues, and it is significant to notice how different is the audience to which he appeals from that of Wycherley or Congreve. The genuine intrusion of middle-class values into the drama comes with George Lillo (1693-1739), whose *The London Merchant or The History of George Barnwell* depicts the life of an apprentice with all the seriousness which in the earlier drama had been restricted to those of rank. The play, with its moral emphasis and its melodramatic theme, made a wide and immediate appeal. It was recognized that a new element had entered into drama, even if the dramatist introducing it was obviously not of the first rank. The innovation is far more important than the play which introduces it, for this way leads to the modern social and realistic drama.

The depths of sentimentalism were reached by dramatists such as Hugh Kelly and Richard Cumberland. The curious can turn to such a play as Cumberland's *The West Indian* (1771) to find how every human issue can be obscured in the welter of emotion. From such depths the drama was rescued by Goldsmith and Sheridan. Oliver Goldsmith (1728-74) might have been one of the greatest figures of our literature if he had only taken more pains. His early play *The Good Natured Man* (1768) reads feebly now, though its intentions of mocking the excesses of false charity are obvious. *She Stoops to Conquer* (1773) has clung to the stage, and particularly to the amateur stage, until the present day. In a way it is the great example of comedy of amateur genius in the language. It goes back to the atmosphere of Farquhar's *Beaux' Stratagem*, and brings back a breath of genuine humanity to a drama stifled with excessive emotions. Its plot, though recklessly improbable, is adequate to maintain the humour of the situation and the bluntly clear delineation of the characters. Hardcastle and Tony Lumpkin are at once types and individuals and, like all the great comic characters, images of their age, and yet recognizable as human figures once the fashion of their own time has disappeared. Far more distinction attaches to the comedy of Richard Sheridan (1751-1816), who in his extraordinary career was at one time Under-Secretary for Foreign Affairs and Secretary to the Treasury. Unfortunately he was early distracted from his career as a dramatist, so that his fame depends on three comedies, *The Rivals* (1775), *The School for Scandal* (1777), and *The Critic* (1779). With Sheridan something of the brilliance of Restoration dialogue returned into comedy, though without the narrow and immoral Restoration world. Instead, a more genial and romantic atmosphere is created, as if some memories of Shakespeare were descending into eighteenth-century Bath.

The characters are firmly presented, with clarity reminiscent of Jonson, though the atmosphere in Sheridan is gayer. Some concessions to sentimentalism he felt bound to make, but the ironic spectator need not treat them too seriously. There is no depth in Sheridan's world, no new interpretation of human nature. In this he is nearer to Wilde than to Jonson. It must always be remembered how short was his career as a dramatist. *The Rivals* shows an ease and mastery which in a first play is almost incredible. Already in *The School for Scandal* he has improved on this brilliant beginning, both in the balance of the action and the technical perfection of the scenes. The main memory from his plays is of the verbal dexterity and the laughter which his well-planned scenes can create. Distinctive his comedy undoubtedly is, though its quality cannot easily be described. Often its make-up seems derived and yet the whole is strikingly individual. He was sufficiently realistic to portray the late eighteenth century as no other dramatist had done, yet with the geniality of romance. He is unembarrassed by any message, unless it be that the generous and open-hearted spirit is in life the most commendable. It may be that the recognition of this quality has added to the enjoyment which successive generations of audiences have found in his plays.

CHAPTER EIGHT

ENGLISH DRAMA FROM SHERIDAN TO G. B. SHAW

THE drama of the early nineteenth century was on the whole deplorable. While poetry and fiction were drawing upon the genius of the romantics, the theatre was the home mainly of irregular spectacle, melodrama, and farce. Even the revivals of the more creditable drama of earlier ages were presented with but little taste or understanding. Most of the romantic poets attempted drama, but with little success. The one outstanding exception was, surprisingly, Shelley's *The Cenci* (1820) though the theme of incest made the play impossible for the stage. A number of reasons have been assigned to this decay of the drama. A simple external reason can be found in the monopoly held by the two houses, Covent Garden and Drury Lane, for the performance of serious drama. They had become too large for the subtle effects of the actor's art, and the managers had been led to numerous expedients to maintain solvency. The Act of 1843 for regulating the theatre removed the monopoly and allowed the smaller theatres to produce drama equally with the two patent houses. As a result, in the sixties, a number of new theatres were built in London.

The decline of the drama cannot be assigned to any single cause. The prosperous middle-class society had no genuine appreciation for drama as an art, and the actor, with a few notable exceptions, remained a member of a profession without honour. The audiences which gathered to the nineteenth-century theatre had not the intelligence, or the imagination, of the Elizabethan audiences. The State certainly looked with bleak unconcern upon the art, which should be a central one in any healthy national life. Neither the Court, nor the Queen, had the talent to encourage drama, and so commercialism, which was infecting England in many other ways, dominated the theatre.

The danger in the nineteenth-century theatre was, above all, that it was unrelated to the life of the time. The changes in the structure of society had so modified the human personality itself that a new interpretation was essential. Lillo in the eighteenth century had a dim recognition of this, but he had inadequate powers as a dramatist, and no one followed his lead. In England, in the nineteenth century, the most valiant attempt to bring the drama closer to life is found in the comedies of T. W. Robertson (1829-71), of which the best remembered is *Caste*. When read, the play seems crude and vulgar, with sentimentality and melodrama corrupting the vision of comedy, but, on the stage, the whole comes to life: the characters live, the action seems real, and often very moving. First produced in 1867, with a number of new devices in the actual presentation, *Caste* is a great advance, though when it is remembered that Ibsen wrote *Peer Gynt* the same year one is reminded of the danger of confusing talent with genius. Much has been written of the influence of Ibsen on the English drama, but apart from G. B. Shaw it is difficult to find anyone who accepted the full influence of the great Norwegian. His work towers over all that the English stage has produced in the modern period: with his poetical plays, *Brand* and *Peer Gynt*, we have nothing even to offer in comparison, while his social and psychological dramas from *The Doll's House*, *Ghosts*, and *An Enemy of the People* to *When We Dead Awaken* are far more subtle in stagecraft, and profound in thought, than anything in the modern English theatre.

The descent from Ibsen to Henry Arthur Jones and Sir A. W. Pinero is a steep one. Both combined a keen estimate of what would constitute a commercial success with a desire to give their audience the deeper effects, which they knew drama could achieve. It is true that Jones's most popular play was a melodrama, *The Silver King*, but he did attempt 'problem' themes in such plays as *Saints and Sinners* and *Mrs. Dane's Defence*. Compared with Ibsen, these are the work of an amateur cobbler, who has never mastered his tools. Pinero was more adroit in handling the mechanism of the stage, though, again, compared with Ibsen, he is a bungler. He attempts to deal with real situations, though most of them have an odd air of theatricality. His best-known play, and one of the most effective, is the once notorious *The Second Mr. Tanqueray*, which treats of the marriage of 'a woman with a past.' The return of intelligence to the theatre can be seen more clearly in the comic operas of Gilbert and Sullivan. Their work seems to prepare the audience for the comedy of Oscar Wilde and G. B. Shaw. Wilde (1856-1900) had been ridiculed by Gilbert in *Patience*, but as a writer of comedy he shared with Gilbert a verbal wit, which had been dead on the English stage since Sheridan. His imprisonment, in 1895, for homosexual practices, was a disaster to the theatre. In four comedies, *Lady Windermere's Fan* (1892), *A Woman of No Importance* (1893), *An Ideal Husband* (1895), and *The Importance of being Earnest* (1895), he had shown not only his own brilliance but the rapidity with which he was progressing in his art. A certain number of the dreary-minded have failed to recognize his wit which had to exercise itself on the few themes permitted by the squeamishness of his audience.

The twentieth century showed a talent in the drama with which the nineteenth century could not compete. H. Granville Barker and Vedrenne produced seasons of plays at the Court Theatre, which brought an enlightenment into production, and a discipline into acting. Granville Barker was himself a dramatist who explored contemporary problems with a brave and unyielding realism in a number of plays, which include *The Voysey Inheritance* (1905), and *Waste* (1907). He is prepared to exploit grimness and despair, though it can be seen from *The Marrying of Ann Leete* that he had a romantic element, and this appears again more obviously in *Prunella*, where he collaborated with Laurence Housman. John Galsworthy (1867-1933), who was actually a better artist as a novelist than as dramatist, also based his plays on social and contemporary problems. His success with audiences in the theatre began with *Strife* (1909) and *Justice* (1910) and continued in a number of later plays, including *Loyalties* (1922). He seems sometimes to have formulated his selected social problem rather blatantly, and his characterization is simple, while the theme is pressed home with a heavy emphasis. Though his plays are well constructed, the mechanism tends to remain apparent. His sense of pity was controlled usually by his intelligence, but it was always in danger of becoming excessive. St. John Ervine in his earlier plays, notably in *Jane Clegg* (1913) and *John Ferguson* (1915), continued the realistic tradition with great sincerity, and with less obvious intentions. Further, John Masefield, in *The Tragedy of Nan* (1908), gave a poetic quality to domestic realism which is reminiscent of seventeenth-century drama.

St. John Ervine had been associated with a group of Irish dramatists, whose work was normally produced in the Abbey Theatre in Dublin. Much that is best in the modern drama in English developed from this movement. One of its originators was Lady Gregory, who was herself a dramatist. W. B. Yeats was led to bring his poetical gift to the service of the movement, and though he remains a lyrical writer rather than a dramatist, some of his plays, such as *The Countess Cathleen* (1892) and *The Land of Heart's Desire* (1894), do evoke the mysticism and folk-lore of the Irish imagination. Greater as a dramatist was John Millington Synge (1871-1909), who had travelled widely on the Continent before he was encouraged by Yeats to seek in the Aran Islands a new and simple language for drama. His *Playboy of the Western World* (1907) is a comic interpretation of Irish character, governed by a deep, even poetical, understanding. In tragedy, his short play, *Riders to the Sea*, in which a mother acknowledges the dark power of the fate that will destroy her last son, has a Greek quality, combined with a simplicity befitting its peasant setting. *Deirdre of the Sorrows*, the play upon which he was working at the time of his death, shows what a loss the theatre suffered when he died before he was forty. That the Irish drama did not die with Synge can be seen in the work of Sean O'Casey, who, in *Juno and the Paycock* and *The Shadow of a Gunman*, has portrayed the life of Dublin as vividly as earlier dramatists had shown Irish peasant life.

The English drama was not confined to the social realism of Granville Barker and Galsworthy. It is the fashion today to despise Sir James Barrie, but it is dangerous to despise a man who invented a mythology and added to the English stage a play that will be permanent. This Barrie did in *Peter Pan* (1904). The sentimentality of this fantasy, full of the folk-lore of childhood, becomes less acceptable when extended to ordinary life, but this need not disguise the fine craftsmanship of plays such as *The Admirable Crichton* (1902), and *Dear Brutus* (1917).

All else in the modern theatre must take second place to the achievement of George Bernard Shaw. His career has been the longest in English dramatic history; beginning with *Widowers' Houses* in 1892 it continues to 1939 with *In Good King Charles's Golden Days*. Shaw first entered the theatre as a dramatic critic, and the volumes of *Our Theatre in the Nineties* show his brilliant commentary on the stage of that period. His intellectual equipment was far greater than that of any of his contemporaries. He alone had understood the greatness of Ibsen, and he was determined that his own plays should also be a vehicle for ideas. His temperament had nothing of Ibsen's grimness. If he saw, with unusual clarity, the ills of the world, he possessed an inalienable Irish capacity for jest and a verbal wit equal to that of Congreve or Wilde. The combination of wide social enthusiasms with a gift for comedy was, to say the least, unusual, and it is thus that Shaw's plays have a quality all their own.

William Archer has described Shaw, as a young man, sitting in the British Museum Reading Room, with Marx's *Das Kapital* and the score of *Tristan und Isolde* set out before him. The picture is not an unfair image of his work. If he had Socialism, the Fabian Society, sex, ethics, religion as themes crowding up for admission into his plays, he had also a genuine artistic gift for form. He was impatient of clumsy workmanship in the theatre, though for him mechanical perfection is not enough: to compare his comedies with Jones's or Pinero's is to realize at once his advance in construction and in the management of his characters. His originality had tended to obscure these more ordinary virtues, but his own essays show how closely he had studied every detail of theatrical workmanship.

In the early plays the originality lay largely in the conception of character. He would take a conventional stage type, reverse it, and then prove that the reversal was the truth. Thus, in *Arms and the Man*, for the romantic stage soldier he substitutes the mercenary, who knows fear and hunger; in *Mrs. Warren's Profession* he replaces the romantic courtesan with the woman who is conducting the profitable, but unpleasant, trade of prostitution. Also, he allowed his characters to speak all of what was in their minds, however disconcerting it might be.

This reversal of the ordinary conception of character has remained the most consistent feature of his satirical comedy, and he has employed it in plays from *Caesar and Cleopatra* to *St. Joan*. It gave his drama a vague classical quality, akin to the 'humours' characterization of Jonson.

He had, from the first, accepted a burden in his dramas, beyond the presentation of plot and character. He had signed a contract with himself, and with the spirit of Ibsen, that each play should present a problem and discuss it thoroughly. Character, thus, never comes first in his plays, and, among the early comedies, in *Candida* (1894) alone, where he follows Ibsen in championing woman's freedom, does he show a character who is memorable apart from the sentiments she has to convey. Aristotle gave plot an importance in drama before characterization, and so does Shaw, but for a different reason. His fable must be so chosen that it will allow him to discuss the theme he has set himself. Some critics suggest that his plays have no plot. If so, Mr. Shaw is cleverer even than he is reported to be. Actually, the conception of plot varies from one play to another. Sometimes, he approaches the ordinary story plot, as in *The Devil's Disciple*, or in *St. Joan*, but occasionally he reduces the story to a minimum as in *Getting Married*. Probably the most acceptable plays of the middle period were those in which he discovered a balance between the two methods, as in *Major Barbara*, or *The Shewing-up of Blanco Posnet*, or *John Bull's Other Island*. Though he used his plays for discussion, he accompanied them with prefaces in which he explored the themes more fully. In some instances, as for example, *Androcles and the Lion*, with its prefatory essay on Christianity, the major burden of the discussion has been left to the preface. On the whole, the later plays of the post-war period, *Heartbreak House* (1920), *The Apple Cart* (1929), *Too True to Be Good* (1932), *The Millionairess* (1936), and *Geneva* (1938) have shown an increase of discussion, with very great skill in using a pattern of plot to keep the talk in sound dramatic order.

It is difficult to gain any just perspective in estimating a great contemporary figure. Whether Shaw survives or not is a matter for posterity. The brilliant philosophical comedy of *Man and Superman* has already lost something of its first dazzling freshness, and the same is true of *Back to Methuselah*. Neither has the same survival value as *Pygmalion*, in which Shaw gives a human and modern presentation of the old fairy-tale theme of the poor little girl who is transformed into a lady. When a writer has given his generation so much it is wrong to complain, and wrong to have regrets. One can but express the wish that he had not suppressed the romantic element in himself so completely. In *St. Joan* it colours his work, and occasionally he makes use of 'fancy dress' devices in the other plays, as if he had suddenly persuaded himself of the necessity for colour.

His greatest gift was his verbal wit. It was also his greatest temptation. To some he seems only a mental mountebank who enjoyed railing at the things which others respected, or held sacred. Such a view is obviously false. Much in the plays is fiercely serious, and the prefaces are all arguments, conducted with honesty and close reasoning. Comedy was not idleness with him, but the weapon with which he fought the inert and compact majority. The warning, which he extended to his generation, was in most ways unanswerable. Civilized man must either develop or perish, as the primeval beasts had perished before him. 'The Life Force,' or God, would not tolerate that man should continue with his cruelty, his corruption, and ineffectuality. That central theme he illustrated through every phase of life, from education and social conditions, to politics, international affairs, and religion. That he has had a profound effect need not be denied, but there remains a suspicion that the message would have been clearer if the wit had been less. Our age needed a new Aquinas and we were given G. B. Shaw. Without humour, the vision of life as he saw it would have led him to the scaffold as a revolutionary. Perhaps some future age, looking back on this time, will feel that it would have been better had it been so, though, of course, Mr Shaw has a right to his own opinions on this, as on other matters, and he has already expressed them.

With Shaw, any brief study of the English theatre may with justice end, but there are a number of his contemporaries who have written with distinction. Somerset Maugham had written for the stage as early as 1898 and has composed over thirty plays mainly of a satirical 'madness' comedy, of which the most notable is *The Circle* (1921). Noel Coward showed himself a great master of the whole machinery of the modern stage from the comedy of *Fallen Angels* (1925) to the spectacle of *Cavalcade*. More original than either of these was 'James Bridie' (Dr Mavor) whose plays such as *The Anatomist* and *Tobias and the Angel* had comedy into an original and sometimes fantastic imagination. Meanwhile in the thirties J. B. Priestley invaded the theatre after his success in fiction and liked it so much that he decided to stay. It is too early as yet to attempt to place Mr T. S. Eliot as a dramatist in the story of English drama as a whole. *Murder in the Cathedral* (1935) is an interesting experiment in verse tragedy to which both classical drama and 'Morality' play had given suggestions. A note must also be made of the experiments of W. H. Auden and Christopher Isherwood in *The Dance of Death* (1933) and *The Ascent of F6* (1936). They attempt to release drama from prose and from argument, by a use of dancing and mime, and they employ stage effects not unlike those used by the German expressionists. None of these authors finds much acceptance in the commercial theatre. To read the list of plays offered by the London theatre in the early months of the war in 1939 was to feel that the stage was moribund. This is not so. We have actors, and if playwrights are not plentiful, we have an ample number of plays to produce, or revive. The commercial theatre of London is a corruption of the drama. Against it a few theatres have maintained a standard, and in the provinces the Repertory Theatres, despite their puny resources, have been admirable. It is promising to note that since the Second World War the State, through the Arts Council of Great Britain, has given assistance to the Arts, and this may well mark the beginning of a new age in the theatre.

CHAPTER NINE

THE ENGLISH NOVEL TO DEFOE

THE story is the most widely distributed form of literature. Epic, ballad, anecdote, romance, they are all stories. At the same time, the novel as we know it today is a late growth, and a special form of story-telling: some would place its origins in the eighteenth century with Richardson's *Pamela*. Certainly it cannot, in England, be traced back earlier than the sixteenth century, with Sir Philip Sidney's *Arcadia*, and most modern readers would feel that this work fulfilled few of the requirements of a novel. It is necessary, then, to distinguish the novel from story-telling. The novel is a prose work, while most of the early story-telling was in verse. Chaucer's *Troilus and Criseyde* has many of the things a modern reader would expect in a novel, except that Chaucer writes in verse. Verse returns into popularity from time to time as a method of story-telling. Scott and Byron in their verse romances had the last popular success of this kind; but Scott showed that prose gives possibilities of width and background to the story, with which verse cannot compete. Width and background are two ways in which the novelist distinguishes his art from that of the story-teller. He is not only telling a story, but portraying something through the story. Along with the story, the novel gives a portrait of character, or of social background. Whatever ambition governs the novelist, he will do well to remember that he began as a story-teller, and that origin he can never altogether escape. Thus the novel can be described as a narrative in prose, based on a story, in which the author may portray character, the life of an age, analyse sentiments and passions, and the reactions of men and women to their environment. This he may do either with a setting of his own times, or of the past. Further, beginning with a setting in ordinary life he may use the novel for fantasy, or a portrayal of the supernatural.

The novel may be the last form of literature to establish itself, but since the eighteenth century its success has been almost alarming. In the 'circulating libraries,' fiction has its own methods of distribution, and already in the eighteenth century there are frequent complaints about the excessive amount of time spent in novel-reading. Yet this attachment of a large public to the novel is not surprising. For many it is the only outlet to a large experience. For others it is an indirect satisfaction of some need for a philosophical or moral guidance not set out in rules, but worked out, experimentally, in the portrayal of conduct. Apart from all this, the novelist's art is a great one, touching life everywhere, and using not only description, but the dramatist's gift of dialogue. It is the form in literature which has explored most fully the life of the ordinary man, and found it worthy of portrayal. For some reason, it is the form of literature in which women have competed successfully with men, and the novel of the future may lie more with woman than with man. It is probable that the reading public for the novel today contains a majority of women.

Though it is a great art, it is also an art which admits of much mediocre talent. The history of the novel is difficult to describe, because the number of novels is so great. Stated generally, the history of the novel shows an increase in complexity, and a growing dissatisfaction with the story merely as a story. The different types of novel cannot be easily defined, for they are so many. Probably the most valuable distinction is between the novel which deals with the writer's own age, as H. G. Wells did in *Tono Bungay*, and the novel which uses an historical setting. The former is often realistic, and the latter frequently incorporates adventure of the spectacular kind. This realistic and contemporary novel is slower in its growth historically than the romance, but once it develops it has a great hold on the public imagination. In itself, it has many divisions, almost as many as Polonius's divisions of the drama in *Hamlet*: comic in *Pickwick Papers*; sociological in Charles Reade's *Never Too Late to Mend*; philosophical in Meredith's *Diana of the Cross-*

ways. The other convenient division of the novel is according to form, and here the complexity is no less great. The novelist may tell a story in a straightforward manner, narrating events in their chronological order. Few novelists have been satisfied with this, though some writers, such as Anthony Trollope, seem to gain by ordering the narrative in as simple a way as possible. With some novelists, the form of the narrative holds the attention first, as in Sterne's *Tristram Shandy*, and Sterne is a precursor of the modern novelists who have experimented with form, notably Dorothy Richardson, James Joyce, and Virginia Woolf. The experiment need not be so extreme as in these writers, or so deliberate. Thomas Love Peacock and Aldous Huxley have both, in separate but allied ways, departed from plain narrative to make the novel a vehicle for ideas and conversation. In the eighteenth century, Richardson discovered by accident that the best way in which he could give his analysis of sentiment in the novel was by letters. One returns here to the realization that the novel is a mixed form. When the novelist uses dialogue and reduces description to a minimum he approaches drama. Jane Austen's *Pride and Prejudice* contains all the essential dialogue for a play on that theme, and so does Meredith's *The Egoist*. At the other extreme, the novel draws towards the essay and the discourse, in such reflective works as Walter Pater's *Marius the Epicurean*.

In the pages that follow, the history of the English novel has been traced through the works which seem most clearly to show these aspects of its development. The beginning, though it is no beginning, can be made with Sir Philip Sidney (1554-86) at Wilton, the beautiful house of his sister, the Countess of Pembroke, writing *The Countess of Pembroke's Arcadia*, for the purpose of amusing his friends. This is a complex romance, of shipwrecked princes, beautiful princesses, chivalric adventures, and a pastoral setting, an ideal world, the day-dream of a courtier. It remained popular until the eighteenth century, and when Richardson, the bourgeois printer, named his serving-maid heroine, he called her 'Pamela,' in memory of a character in Sidney's story. A very different work came at the same time from that very brilliant young Cambridge man, John Lyly (1554-1606), who would be better remembered also as a writer of comedies had not Shakespeare followed him so closely. His *Euphues* (1579), and his *Euphues and his England*, reduce story to a minimum, but they are brilliant in the discussion of manners, sentiment, and moral reflection. Some of his matter he borrowed from Castiglione's *The Courtier*, an Italian guide-book to gentlemanly behaviour. Lyly dedicated his work to the ladies of England, a prophetic anticipation of the large number of women readers the novel was to possess. A third group of Elizabethan writers, who lived much lower down the social scale, wrote for money, though, as their lives suggest, the payments must have been small, despite all their efforts to follow popular taste. Robert Greene (1560-92), dramatist, pamphleteer, poet, and Bohemian, wrote a number of pieces in which he merely popularized the effects of Sidney and Lyly. These included *Pandosto* (1585), which Shakespeare used for *The Winter's Tale*. He also developed a manner of his own in describing the 'low' life of Elizabethan London, the thieves, rogues, drabs, their tricks, and their victims. Thomas Lodge (1558-1625) also tried fiction both ways, with a story in Sidney's manner, entitled *Rosalynde* (1590), and with realistic pamphlets. More entertaining is Thomas Deloney (1543-1600), who describes the work of craftsmen, in narratives that are simple, anachronistic, but grounded in realism. In *Jack of Newbury* he shows the life of the weavers, and in *The Gentle Craft* he tells the whole story of the shoemakers, with some vivid and seemingly authentic scenes. With these Thomas Dekker, who was also a dramatist, portrayed contemporary life in a number of tracts, of which the most successful is *The Gull's Horn-Book*, in which the 'low' life of London is paraded.

Realistic though these writers were they had little form in their narratives, but some progress in this direction is made by Thomas Nashe (1567-1601). In *Jack Wilton* he constructed a chronicle of adventures, many of which he had encountered in his own stormy career. His rogue hero begins his career in the army of Henry VIII, and in his travels meets a number of living people. Here was the nearest approach to the realistic novel which the sixteenth century had produced.

It is strange and unaccountable that these beginnings of fiction in the Elizabethan age do not develop, as might be expected, in the seventeenth century. The religious controversies, the social dissensions, and ultimately the Civil Wars, left a trail of innumerable pamphlets, and some have thought that the energies so absorbed left no leisure for prose fiction. Yet the early seventeenth century is not without its contribution to the history of fiction. The most important new element came from France in the elegant, far-fetched, and interminable heroic romances of Mlle de Scudery, whose *Le Grand Cyrus* was translated in 1653-5 and proved popular. The primary appeal of these romances was to the aristocracy, but others enjoyed them. Sentiment, character, and theme were all elevated and idealized in a prose imitation of the Greek heroic poetry and the Greek romances. These volumes dealt with adventures entirely removed from ordinary life, and in attempting to describe them Englishmen first began to use the word 'romantic.'

The second half of the seventeenth century had more numerous developments. If the novel itself made little progress, we do begin to hear the voice of the private citizen describing his own life. Samuel Pepys and John Evelyn, in their diaries, are recording the type of material which novelists were one day to use. The attitude to life, from which came their observation of the everyday detail of existence, is developing the atmosphere which one day is to make fiction so acceptable.

The greatest fiction writer of the seventeenth century, and one of the great figures in our literature, who would have himself disclaimed all title to being a novelist, was John Bunyan (1628-88). Son of a Bedfordshire tradesman, he was a soldier in the Republican Army, a preacher, a prisoner, and mystic. His earliest work is his moving spiritual autobiography, *Grace Abounding* (1666). The first part of *The Pilgrim's Progress*, written during one of his terms of imprisonment, was published in 1678, and a second part followed in 1684. Equally effective, though less well known, were *The Life and Death of Mr Badman* (1680), the counterpart to the story of the good pilgrim; and the spacious and magnificent *Holy War* (1682). When modern critics look for the proletarian writer they forget that Bunyan is our supreme example, and it is well to remember that he was not concerned with the class-struggle but with the struggle for a man's soul, which for centuries in our literature seemed vastly more important. Without regular education, and undisturbed by literary traditions, he had before him one great model of prose in the English Bible. From his religious meditation he gained the supreme experience of man's struggle in the world with sin, and he had that profound sense of evil and guilt in the personality, which is common to most mystics.

In *The Pilgrim's Progress*, he determined to recount the vision of life allegorically, as the narrative of a journey. Allegory may be anything from a dull mechanism to a great and lively work of the imagination. Bunyan was endowed with a gift for detail and anecdote, for the description of scenery and the invention of conversation. This he combined with his allegory, so that his narrative, despite all its spiritual meanings, is a realistic story, contemporary and authentic. The union of this realism with his spiritual experience can be seen by the exactness with which he describes, in *Grace Abounding*, the incidents which led to his conversion. It is useless to look for antecedents for Bunyan's work, though his allegorical method is ultimately medieval: nor can one usefully seek for followers. He was unique, and his work entered into that part of our literature which transcends its age and is permanent.

With all these earlier developments to the novel, it is left to the eighteenth century to consolidate fiction as a form of literature, and from that time onwards there has been no cessation in novel-writing. A beginning is made with an enthralling and mysterious figure, Daniel Defoe (1660-1731), to whom the English public, with all its taste for biography, has never taken kindly. Educated in a Dissenting College at Stoke Newington, Defoe, apart from being an inexhaustible writer, was a Government agent, both for the Whigs and the Tories, and, some suspect, for both at the same time. He was a speculator, an inventor, a bankrupt, a traveller, and a journalist. Once he endured the pillory, and he was on several occasions imprisoned. Though his moral nature was not strong, he kept reserved, very compactly, in one corner of his mind, the Puritan values in which he was educated. Novel-writing was only one of his activities, and he came to it late in life, and rich in experience. Outstanding among his earlier productions is *The Review* (1704-13), which marks the turning-point in the history of our journalism and periodical literature. Apart from the short narrative of the *Apparition of Mrs Veal* (1706), which reads like a work of imagination, but which Defoe wrote from the results of his researches, his first work of fiction is *Robinson Crusoe* (1719). Published when Defoe was sixty, its success encouraged him, and there followed, in rapid succession: *Captain Singleton* (1720); *Moll Flanders* (1722); *Colonel Jacque* (1722); *A Journal of the Plague Year* (1722); and *Roxana* (1724). Defoe's outlook on the novel is best illustrated through *A Journal of the Plague Year*, which was once considered as a work of the imagination constructed from cleverly invented incidents. Actually, apart from a slender fictional centre, it depended on memories of the Plague, which were still circulating in Defoe's childhood, and on his own research among documents. Further, the subject was topical when he wrote, for there was a threatened recurrence of the scourge. He regards the novel, not as a work of the imagination, but as a 'true relation,' and even when the element of fact decreases, he maintains the close realism of pseudo-fact. He writes with a knowledge of his audience, mainly the Puritan middle classes, and selects themes which will have an immediate appeal to them. Superficially, these two conditions would appear to detract from his originality, but there exists in him a talent for organizing his material into a well-conducted narrative, with an effective eye for detail, in a style ever simple and welcoming, but never obtrusive. The combination of these qualities gave *Robinson Crusoe* its immediate and continuous appeal. The story had its basis in fact, in the adventures of Alexander Selkirk, the sailor who lived alone for years on the island of Juan Fernandez, and this initial circumstance is supported by Defoe's wide reading in works of travel, and by his own multifarious experience. The skill of the novel lies in its detail, in the semblance of the authentic. Form, in its subtler sense, does not affect Defoe: his novels run on until, like an alarm clock, they run down; but while movement is there the attention is held. While he has some interest in mental states, Defoe reveals less of the mind of Crusoe than one would expect, and it would be interesting to see how Henry James would have re-told the story. The dullest part of the work lies in the moral and religious reflections, and here Defoe was making use of that part of his mind which retained unadulterated the Puritan values which he had absorbed as a child. Also he knew that his audience would like it. The success of *Robinson Crusoe* obscures the lively merit of the moral, but picaresque, novels which follow. *Captain Singleton*, with piracy and Africa as its background, is a vivid tale, and the 'female rogues,' Moll Flanders and the more elegant Roxana, are among the most lively of his creations.

CHAPTER TEN

THE ENGLISH NOVEL FROM RICHARDSON TO SIR WALTER SCOTT

DEFOE had no contemporary, no immediate successor, and the next development in the novel, and possibly the most important in its whole history in England, comes by accident. Samuel Richardson (1689-1761), the son of a joiner, came to London, and was apprenticed as a printer. He remained a printer throughout his life, and followed the path of the virtuous and successful apprentice, even to marrying his master's daughter. He was asked to prepare a series of model letters for those who could not write for themselves. Richardson told maid-servants how to negotiate a proposal of marriage, apprentices how to apply for situations, and even sons how to plead their father's forgiveness. This humble task taught Richardson that he had at his fingers' ends the art of expressing himself in letters, and in the years that followed he published three long works, on which his reputation rests: *Pamela* (1740); *Clarissa* (1747-8), and *Sir Charles Grandison* (1753-4).

In each instance, the central story is a simple one. Pamela was a virtuous servant, who resisted the attempts at seduction of the son of her late mistress, and, as a reward, gained from him a proposal of marriage, which she gleefully accepted. Clarissa, again, was virtuous, but a lady. Tormented by the pressure of her family, who urged on her a detestable suitor, she fled from home to the protection of the attractive Mr. Lovelace, who, once he had her in his power, declared his attention in a manner which even her virtuous upbringing could not mistake. Nor was he content with declarations. For when these failed, he forced himself upon her, and, as an indirect consequence of his actions, she died. Sir Charles Grandison was a model gentleman, who rescued one lady, and was betrothed to another, a situation which he controlled with incredible delicacy, to the apparent satisfaction of all parties.

From the outset, the themes of Richardson's novels have been attacked on account of their self-satisfied and calculating middle-class morality. Pamela is accused of having made virtue pay dividends by marriage, and even Clarissa is alleged only to have reserved payment for another world, making a long-term investment with eternity, while Sir Charles, despite his aristocratic glamour, is a prig. Judged merely as a writer of stories, Richardson would not stand high, but, as has already been suggested, the novel is a story told in a special way. It is Richardson's 'special way' that declares his genius. The novelty of form, by which he revealed his narrative through letters, came by accident, but, though never self-conscious in his art, he must have realized that this was his ideal method. For his strength lay in the knowledge of the human heart, in the delineation of the shades of sentiment, as they shift and change. and the cross-purposes which trouble the mind moved by emotion. Lyly had a little of this in *Euphues*, and Chaucer much of it in *Troilus and Criseyde*, and Richardson is in their tradition. In Richardson this analysis of sentiment becomes the dominant motive, and is pursued with a minuteness and patience which the art of fiction in England was seldom to parallel. Content with his humble servants, and his middle-class figures, he evoked the minute incidents of their lives, through which their emotions were realized, with the absolute clarity of a master. Nor were the moral and religious values, which affected adversely the themes themselves, without their value, for they allowed him to see in the detailed incident an importance arising from its spiritual significance. His realism in narration was combined with a skill in dialogue which has seldom had its due recognition. Nor, as might be imagined, is the portrait one of continuous gloom: liveliness, pleasantries, even wit, intervene, But the mastery exists in the absolute integrity of the picture of sentiment and of pathos. Richardson was an artist and a Puritan, and, while the Puritan invents the stories, the artist is in almost absolute control of the detail. Criticism has often been too content to mock at the stories without recognizing the great master who controls their slow and deliberate unravelling. Nowhere in English criticism has Richardson had complete recognition of the greatness of his art.

Richardson has suffered from the appearance of a contemporary of genius who disliked his work, and who took an early opportunity of satirizing it. Henry Fielding (1707-54) was of an aristocratic family, educated at Eton and Leyden, a reader with a wide and genuine taste for the classics, and a dramatist, until Sir Robert Walpole's Licensing Act of 1737 drove his plays from the stage. He was a journalist, a lawyer, and a Justice of the Peace serving at Bow Street.

In 1742 he published *Joseph Andrews*, to ridicule Richardson's *Pamela*. He contrived this satire by reversing the situation in Richardson's novel. Instead of the virtuous serving-maid Fielding presents Joseph, the chaste servant, whom Lady Booby so tempts from the path of virtue that he has to run away. At this moment in the story, Fielding became so engrossed in his own narrative, and the exercise of his own comic gift, that Richardson is almost forgotten. There follows a series of adventures on the road, where Joseph is accompanied by Parson Adams, a clerical Don Quixote. The comedy is admirably contrived, with the Hogarthian figure of a pig-keeping parson as one of its main delights. Fielding's purpose in this first novel is nowhere a simple or direct one. Apart from the motive of satire, he is attracted, in a learned way, by the contrasts between the novel, with its picture of humble, contemporary life, and the classical epic. With this in mind he calls his novel ' a comic epic in prose,' and it leads him, with encouragement from Cervantes, to introduce a burlesque element into the style and frequently into the incident. It was the motive of satire which completely dominated his second narrative, *The History of Jonathan Wild the Great* (1743), in which he took the life of a thief and receiver, who had been hanged at Tyburn, as a theme for demonstrating the small division between a great rogue and a great soldier, or a great politician, such as Sir Robert Walpole.

Underlying the humours of *Joseph Andrews* there lay a view of life, seldom disclosed openly, but of obvious importance to Fielding himself. It could be discovered in the difference between the calculating moral code of Richardson, and the generous and warm-hearted approach to life which Fielding admired. When Joseph lay naked on the roadside, all the members of a passing coach, good Richardsonians, would neglect him from some motive of prudence or modesty, all except a coach-boy, afterwards deported for robbing a hen-roost, who threw him his coat, with an oath. The contemplation of the more intricate relations of good and evil, and the anomaly that generous impulses frequently exist in those whom society condemns, grew in Fielding with such emotional intensity that they gave a depth to his second novel, *Tom Jones* (1749). Nothing in his work compares with this great novel, so carefully planned and executed, that though the main theme follows Tom Jones's life from childhood onwards, the reader is kept in suspense until the close as to the final resolution of the action.

Fielding's last novel, *Amelia* (1751), is not such a consistent success. He idealizes the main woman character, and this leads to an excess of pathos, depriving the novel of the balance which *Tom Jones* possesses. Yet, with Fielding, the novel had come of age. He had established it in one of its most notable forms, middle-class realism. He had endowed it with a conception of form, and made it an art not unworthy of comparison with the pictorial art of Hogarth. In Tom Jones he had drawn one of the great human characters of our literature. Background alone was lacking, and was to remain absent until Scott gave it lavishly in his fictions. Above all, he had less reticence than Richardson, or than any of his successors in the nineteenth century.

Tobias Smollett (1721-71) was Fielding's contemporary, though he is not of equal stature. Born in Scotland, he studied medicine, and served on a warship as a ship's surgeon. If he brought to the novel nothing that was new in form, he was able to introduce a new background, in accounts of the sea in the livid days of the old Navy. Irascible and insensitive, he had an apparent enjoyment of the rough naval life, of its cruelty and the wild practical joking. To this he added, in a rather incongruous way, a superficial element of sentiment.

In his first novel, *Roderick Random* (1748), he portrays the life of his rogue-hero until his marriage with the loyal, beautiful, and incredible Narcissa. The picture of the reckless and ferocious sea life in this novel is his most solid claim to be remembered. *Peregrine Pickle* (1751) is, again, the novel of a rogue who follows a depraved life until he marries the virtuous Emilia. More attractive than this 'hero' are some of the minor characters such as Commodore Trunnion and Boatswain Pipes. The background is still vividly drawn and includes a picture of the cruelties of pre-Revolutionary France. With these two novels Smollet had exhausted his own experience, and in *Ferdinand Count Fathom* (1753) he draws a fantastic villain, who seems an anticipation of the figures in the 'novel of terror' which was soon to follow. Smollett salves his conscience by portraying a moral regeneration before the close. The rest of his work is less impressive: *Sir Lancelot Greaves* (1762) is an eighteenth-century English version of *Don Quixote;* in *Humphrey Clinker* (1771) he modifies Richardson's epistolary manner, and writes in a more humorous and equable manner than in his earlier novels. Smollett had less intellectual integrity, less depth of vision, than either of his predecessors, but his violent and boisterous stories were widely enjoyed, and in popular estimation he lived long enough to influence Dickens.

Of the eighteenth-century novelists, the strangest, and the most variously judged, is Laurence Sterne (1713-68). The great-grandson of a bishop, and the son of a soldier, he was educated almost in the barrack-room, but he found his way to Cambridge and to a Master's degree. He was ordained, and obtained a living in Yorkshire, but though he read theology and published sermons, he had also studied the works of his 'dear Rabelais and dearer Cervantes.' Even in the eighteenth century, when there were many odd clergymen, Sterne would have stood high in a competition to select the oddest. His *Life and Opinion of Tristram Shandy, Gent.* (1760-7), is a novel without predecessors, but the product of an original mind, and immediately popular. Judged by ordinary story-telling standards *Tristram Shandy* is preposterous. The reader has to wait until the third book before the hero is born, and even then his future life remains undefined. The narrative consists of episodes, conversations, perpetual digressions, excursions in learning, with unfinished sentences, dashes, blank pages, fantastic syntax, caprices in humour, bawdy, and sentiment. In the midst of all this there are characters clearly identifiable: Tristram's father, Corporal Trim, Doctor Slop, and My Uncle Toby, the veteran of Marlborough's campaigns and the clearest source of the sentimental in the novel. At first sight it all seems a perversion, a wanton destruction of form, but to judge thus would be to judge superficially. Sterne is asserting, however indirectly, that the orderly narratives of events, with their time and space realism, have little relation to the disorder of the human mind, where sequence is not logical but incredibly capricious. In *Tristram Shandy* he is led to describe this earth as a planet made up of the sweepings of all the rest, and the incongruity of life, which drove Swift to black moods of satire, affected him also, but in a different way. It accounts for his broad facetiousness, for his Rabelaisianism, his recognition of the comic in the very physical figure of man. Nor is this comedy left in detached aridity. While he laughs at the odd experience which is human life, he feels for mankind, afflicted and suffering. The sentiment frequently seems excessive to the objects which arouse it, for even the fly on My Uncle Toby's plate must be considered as a subject for compassion. To this indulgence in sentiment the name sentimental may be attached, and the term was used by Sterne himself in the title of his *Sentimental Journey* (1761), where he portrays a journey through France with a quieter mood than is present in *Tristram Shandy* and with less display for learning, though the humour that invigorated the earlier work is not forgotten.

After the work of these four masters, the stream of fiction broadens continually, until it reaches the flood with which no single intelligence can contend. Even in the late eighteenth century the developments are too diverse to be easily described. Some works stand alone. Samuel Johnson's *Rasselas* (1759), though nominally an Abyssinian narrative, employs a story only for the sake of a philosophical argument, which is a trenchant attack upon eighteenth-century optimism; it parallels in intention, though not in outward form, the almost contemporary *Candide* of Voltaire. Nor does Oliver Goldsmith's *The Vicar of Wakefield* (1766) belong to any one school. Despite all its coincidences and improbabilities this has remained a popular and individual work. Goldsmith had a gift for comedy and for character, a dramatist's eye for effective situations, and an abundance of sentiment, which arose rather from his own nature than from any literary origin. These he combined with a genuine sensibility for the poor, and for all human sufferings, so that in its prison scenes his narrative anticipates the later social purposes to which the novel was to be directed. Nor were English readers dependent solely on native products for in that free-trade in ideas with France which is continuous throughout the age, a number of French novels were introduced to English readers. Marivaux's *Le Paysan parvenu* and *Marianne* were welcome to those who had enjoyed *Pamela*, while a parallel for the sentimentalism of the English novel could be gained in its lavish use by Rousseau in *La Nouvelle Héloise*. The most direct English successor to Richardson was Fanny Burney (1752-1840), daughter of Charles Burney, the musician, who in her youth was petted and praised by Johnson and Garrick and many other men of distinction. She lived to be a lady-in-waiting to Queen Caroline, and to marry a French emigré, General d'Arblay. *Evelina*, her first and best novel, which took the town by storm in 1778, describes, with admirable illustrative incidents, the entry of a country girl into the gaieties and adventures of London. It can still be read with amusement, though the praises of Johnson, Burke, and Reynolds now seem strangely excessive. To compare Miss Burney with Richardson is to lose critical balance, for Richardson could create, while Miss Burney had only a tenuous store of invention to support her own observation and experience. As a consequence her work, instead of improving, declines. *Cecilia* (1782), though more complex, is less natural and less effective. In *Camilla* (1796), she had already developed her gargantuan syntax, falsely described as an imitation of Johnson's style. In her last novel, *The Wanderer* (1814), her style has become a disease. Her *Diary* and *Letters* show her skill in reporting events with a lively eye for any dramatic incident.

The sentimentalism, which Sterne began, remained popular, and gained its most lachrymose exposition in Henry Mackenzie's *The Man of Feeling* (1771), in which the hero is forever weeping under the stress of some pathetic scene, or emotional excitement. Re-read today the novel seems almost a parody, but it was popular, and though it portrays sentiment with a fantastic excess, the author has a broad humanitarian sympathy, everywhere apparent. If Rousseau is to be discovered as one of the influences on Mackenzie, he was clearly the foremost teacher of Thomas Day, whose incredible life is worth reading, and whose *Sandford and Merton* (1783-9) is still remembered, if only by name. This story of the wealthy boy from Jamaica, corrupted by false kindness and luxury, and the honest farmer's son shows a novel diverted into argument and didactism. Henry Brooke, in *The Fool of Quality* (1766-70), provided another of these educational novels in which two personalities are contrasted. Though he may have derived much from Rousseau, he represented sufficiently a growing humanitarianism to attract the attention of Wesley.

Amid these later eighteenth-century developments, one is notable for the dubious path down which it invited readers and authors to tread. The novel of 'terror,' of the 'Gothic' novel, leads into that underworld of fiction, which continues into the tales of horror and crime so popular today. Whatever may be its value by any artistic standard, the 'terror' tale attracted strong minds, and its influence worked upwards, into the higher regions of art, affecting the composition of Scott, and the Brontës, and the poetry of Shelley.

The origin of this type of fiction can be ascribed to *The Castle of Otranto* (1762), of Horace Walpole (1717-97). Horace, son of Sir Robert Walpole, knew much of the great world which his father so long dominated. But his mind, brilliant without deep convictions, was wearied by the intrigue and perpetual search for power that surrounded him. Fortified by number of sinecures, he indulged himself in antiquarianism, and a numerous acquaintance, which included Gray, the poet.

Of his life he has left a record in a voluminous correspondence, one of the most varied and entertaining collections of letters in our language. His antiquarianism had its emotional aspects, for he is the clearest example in the eighteenth century of a widespread sensibility, particularly among men of wealth and leisure, arising from a disillusionment with the increase in commercialism and rationalism in their time. A release was sought in allowing the imagination to contemplate, in solitude, the relics of medieval art to be found in the ruins of abbeys and castles, often existing within a gentleman's own estate. The same longing for the antique world led to the revival of a taste for ballads and chivalry, for the whole wonder and mystery which later generations have found in the Middle Ages. Walpole carried out the medieval cult more completely than most of his contemporaries, and at Strawberry Hill he constructed a Gothic house, where he could dream himself back into the days of chivalry and monastic life. From these medieval daydreams *The Castle of Otranto* resulted. Set in medieval Italy, the story includes a gigantic helmet that can strike dead its victims, tyrants, supernatural intrusions, mysterious and secret terrors. It is as if all the poetry and character had been removed from Shakespeare's *Macbeth*, only to leave the raw mechanism of melodrama and the supernatural. That the story was popular is intelligible, but that Walpole should ever have thought his pasteboard structure a solid and important work of art is difficult to credit. No one could have foreseen how long would be the catalogue of his imitators. William Beckford (1760-1844) was another gentleman of fashion and wealth, who had built himself a Gothic edifice, Fonthill Abbey, and who had written a romance of mystery. As Fonthill was more extravagant than Strawberry Hill, so is *Vathek* (1782) a more bizarre composition than *The Castle of Otranto*. Walpole, though he daydreamed, had a sound sense of the material world, but Beckford seemed actually to live in a territory of fantasy. *Vathek* is an Oriental story of a caliph who pursues his complex cruelties and intricate passions, aided by his mother and supported by an evil genius. Often passages of beauty occur, but the main impression is of a fantastic world of lavish indulgences. Its strength lies in its consistency, and in the suggestion that through the narrative Beckford was giving some image of his own grandiose and perverted mind.

Of the later practitioners of the 'terror' tale the most able and popular was Mrs Ann Radcliffe (1764-1822), of whose five novels the best known are *The Mysteries of Udolpho* (1794) and *The Italian* (1797). She accepted the mechanism of the 'terror' tale, but combined it with sentiment and with sentimental but effective descriptions of scenery. In this way she brought the 'terror' tale into contact with the interest in nature present in eighteenth-century poetry. *The Mysteries of Udolpho* gives the formula of her work in its most unadulterated form: an innocent and sensitive girl in the hands of a powerful and sadistic villian named Montoni, who owns a grim and isolated castle, where mystery and horror stalk in the lonely corridors and haunted chambers. It is true that before the end of her story Mrs Radcliffe delights in presenting a rational explanation of her horrors. Her work not only attracted the circulating-library readers, who are satirized by Jane Austen in *Northanger Abbey*, but it infected a number of powerful minds. Byron at Newstead Abbey was a Montoni who had come to life, while for Shelley these ghosts of the 'terror' tales became so real that he actually saw them. Charlotte Brontë's Rochester in *Jane Eyre* was only a Montoni modified into a middle-class setting, nor could Emily's great novel *Wuthering Heights* have been written had not her imagination been stimulated from this strange source.

Though Mrs Radcliffe was pre-eminent in her success, many other writers practised this popular manner. Matthew Gregory ('Monk') Lewis (1775-1818), who had read Goethe and the German romanticists, employed all the worst of his reading in *The Monk* (1795). He used a modification of the Faust theme for such a portrayal of sensuality that contemporary taste was offended, though the book was very popular. Lewis followed this notorious success with *Tales of Terror* (1799) and *Tales of Wonder* (1801). Far more honest as an artist was Charles Robert Maturin (1782-1824), whose *Melmoth the Wanderer* (1820) had a wide influence in France. One of the most competent of the 'terror' tales was *Frankenstein* (1817), written by Mrs Shelley with a hint from Byron and Shelley. It is the novel of a mechanical monster, with human powers but of a terrifying aspect. Of all the novels of this type it is the only one that still has a public today.

The nineteenth century was to produce work in fiction of far greater significance than the 'terror' tale. Seldom has the novel been conceived with such deliberate and successful art as in the novels of Jane Austen (1775-1817), daughter of the Rector of Steventon. Her brother served at the Nile and Trafalgar, but her own life was spent at Steventon and Bath, at Chawton and Winchester. From the first she seems to have realized the scene which she could portray, and nothing could tempt her outside. For the past she has no curiosity, and the events which stirred the Europe of her day leave no impression on her pages. In the same manner she detaches herself from the weaknesses of her predecessors. To the 'terror' tale she presented the assault direct, in *Northanger Abbey* (not published until 1817), and she combined with her satire of the 'Gothic' school a deeply studied picture of imaginary horror working in the human mind. The moral outlook of Richardson left her unimpressed, and her art is the more detached for its absence. Sentimentalism found her equally unmoved. Her observation, with whatever difference of scale, has the 'negative capability' of Shakespeare. More than anyone since Fielding, she regarded the novel as a form of art which required a close and exacting discipline. The resulting narratives are so inevitable in their movement, so precise in their realism, that they give the impression of ease, but the facility is a gift to the reader, exacted from the fundamental brainwork of the author. Her integrity as an artist is shown by the fact that she had continued to write and to revise novels, though her work was not at first acceptable to the publishers. *Pride and Prejudice* (1813), which shows her early manner, probably remains her most popular work. The characters are all familiarly known to a wide circle of readers: Mrs Bennet, the match-making mother, Collins, the sycophantic clergyman, the imperious 'great Lady' Catharine de Bourgh, and Elizabeth, the gay, clever young woman whose Prejudice is matched with the Pride of Darcy, the aristocrat who conceals a good-sense of heart beneath a haughty manner and an almost Brahministic power of detecting class distinctions. The narrow circle which her novels were to portray is here defined, the aristocracy and such classes beneath as may, in varying degrees, have some claim upon their intimacy and patronage. Her art exacts in the first place that the novel shall have a classical precision of structure. This central design is manipulated through incidents exactly defined in their realism, and all regulated for their function in the novel as a whole. Added to this is the gift of phrase, humorous, illuminating, economical, through which all is related, so that each incident can be enjoyed in itself, apart from the added pleasure of realizing its true proportion and place in the growing structure of the theme. She had, further, a gift for dialogue, which fails her only in the longer speeches. Background and description she eliminates, except where the balls and parties, the formal calls and visits are necessary for the narrative. *Sense and Sensibility* (1811), her other early volume, again presents two contrasted characters, and there is the same skill in the structure of the plot, though possibly the contemporary flavour of this novel makes it less universal in its appeal.

Three other novels followed, and the critics of Jane Austen have disputed their merit in comparison with her earlier work. *Mansfield Park* was published in 1814, *Emma* in 1816, and *Persuasion* followed in 1817. Without entering into controversy, it can be asserted that these later novels lack the continuous comedy, and the semblance of spontaneity, which *Pride and Prejudice* possesses. In compensation, they have a more complex portrayal of character, a more subtle irony, a deeper, possibly a warmer-hearted attitude to the players on her scene. Jane Austen respected the novel as a great art. In *Northanger Abbey* (1817) she had satirized the 'terror' novel, and in her own work she substituted her cleverly worked realism and comedy. Her letters show how conscious she was of what she was doing, and of her own limitations: 'I must keep to my own style and go on in my own way: and though I may never succeed again in that, I am convinced that I should totally fail in any other.' The complete control of her world gives her work a Shakespearian quality, though the world she controlled was smaller.

Seldom has a single age been presented with two artists of such different range and outlook as Jane Austen and Sir Walter Scott (1771-1832). Never was a writer more generous than Scott to good work among his contemporaries, nor a critic more catholic in his taste. He praised Jane Austen, and distinguished her art from his own 'bow-wow' manner. He was born in Edinburgh, the son of a lawyer, and though he employed himself in the same profession, he had early an enthusiasm for literature, and for the antiquities of Scotland. A series of 'raids' into the Highlands stored his mind with legend, which was to be invaluable to him later as a novelist, and his researches led him to publish *The Minstrelsy of the Scottish Border* (1802-3). From being a collector of poetry he became himself a poet. A series of verse romances, beginning with *The Lay of the Last Minstrel* (1805), rewarded him so well financially that he saw in literature a way of paying for the growing expenditure which the satisfaction of his generous tastes incurred. Of an upright domestic morality, he was apparently free from the entanglements which have encumbered some writers of his imaginative intensity. His weakness lay elswhere, and rose, in part, from the very generosity of his nature. He wished to be a 'laird,' to associate with the aristocracy on terms of equality, and to be the master of his own broad acres.

In satisfaction of this desire he acquired Abbotsford as his home, and even before he was a novelist he was entangled in publishing ventures with the Ballantynes, raising funds to meet his perpetual plans for increasing his mansion and his mania for buying land. Throughout his career as a novelist, this pressure for rapid and successful production pursued him, until he was overtaken by the tragedy of his commitments when in 1826 Constable and the Ballantynes were involved in bankruptcy. It is idle to speculate what sort of an artist he would have been had he not possessed this passion for lavish expenditure. To remove it would be to deny him a part of his nature. It is more profitable to record that his *Journal*, written in the period of the collapse, is the most moving of all his works. Nor is it without interest that his success, combined with his ever-pressing needs, increased the rewards of fiction to the author to a scale without precedent.

Until the later years, this rapidity of production leaves little trace on his composition. If he wrote with a minimum of revision, he still wrote well, and his mind was so crowded with stories, characters, and incidents, that invention came without apparent effort. His energy was phenomenal, and some have suspected that certain of the novels must have been written in his earlier years, and hoarded until he had committed himself to his secret and anonymous profession. His performance is the more remarkable when it is remembered that he combined authorship with a number of legal and official duties, while to his guests at Abbotsford he seemed the gentleman of leisure, ready to while away the vacant hours in sport and entertainment, and the care of his estates. The solution, partial though it must be, lies in the fact that his journeys to the Highlands had stored his memory with the background, and much of the material, from which the best in his fiction was to develop. These had been invaluable years of preparation, though Scott was probably unconscious at the time of the use to which he would later apply them.

Scott, though he had some antecedents, including Maria Edgeworth's picture of Irish life in *Castle Rackrent* (1800), may be said to have invented the historical novel. Instead of the contemporary scene, and the detailed study of middle-class life, he steps back into the past, frequently using well-known characters, and constructing a narrative which is at once an adventure and a pageant of an earlier world. Where Fielding and Jane Austen had been content with characters and their immediate surroundings, Scott invented a background for his scene, with landscape and nature descriptions, and all the picturesque details of past ages. Though the central theme often introduces the leading personalities, the most secure element lies in his pictures of ordinary people, particularly the Scottish peasants, whom he knew so well, and in whose portrayal his notable gift for comedy had free exercise. In variety of scene and in the wealth of characters he equals Shakespeare, and yet when their art is compared much is found missing in Scott. The continual impoverishment of English speech, in its frank description of the passions and the crudities of life, deprives his style of the range which Shakespeare possessed. Nor did he penetrate into the hidden places of his characters' minds. Their conduct and emotions are governed by simple motives. If he is rich in comedy, he approaches tragedy seldom, and with unequal success, nor did his happy nature know the agony of a tormented or thwarted soul. His history, too, is pageantry without a deeper understanding of the institutions which have affected men's lives. It is significant that in his treatment of the Middle Ages, the Church, the dominant institution, escapes consideration. For mystery he had a great gift, sparingly used, but the metaphysical and the mystical leave him untouched.

While it is convenient to use the label 'historical novelist' for Scott, the term, without examination, is misleading. His earliest novel, *Waverley* (1814), dealt with the Jacobite rising of 1745, and though in one sense historical, he was able to formulate the background from the memories of living people whom he had met in the Highlands. This Scottish element, with Jacobitism, the last medieval movement in Europe, as its main theme, is the most secure element in his whole work, and he recurs to it frequently: in *Guy Mannering* (1815); *The Antiquary* (1816); *Old Mortality* (1816); *The Heart of Midlothian* (1818); and *Rob Roy* (1818). In these novels it is difficult to dissociate memory from imagination. These both serve his creative purpose equally, and the central narrative is supported by the strong humanity, and the frequently comic portrayal of lowly Scottish types. When Scott departed from the Scotland which he knew so well into the Middle Ages, he lost much of his power. *Ivanhoe* (1820) and *The Talisman* (1825), a history of the Crusades, were among the most popular of his novels, but they are superficial and theatrical compared with the certainty and depth of the Scottish novels. The same is true, though less obviously, when he crosses the Border to narrate the fortunes of Elizabeth and James I in *Kenilworth* (1821) and *The Fortunes of Nigel* (1822).

Once he had exhausted the popular appeal of a period, he hurried to seek another. Among these novelties a certain pride of place must be given to *Quentin Durward* (1823), which deals with the France of Louis XI, for in that novel he captured the attention of Europe. Never was his narrative more vivid, and in Louis he portrays a character more subtle than is usual with him. In this novel, though he has gone to France, he has taken his Scottish archers with him. More than once he returned from these wanderings, geographical and temporal, to employ Scotland as his scene. *Saint Ronan's Well* (1824), where he experiments with the novel of manners, is interesting without being completely successful, but *Redgauntlet* (1824), in which he bids farewell to the Jacobite theme, shows how Scotland was supremely his subject. In his work as a novelist he has given a wider enjoyment than any writer, with the possible exception of Dickens. Since his day the knowledge of the past has increased, but the inaccuracies in his portraits are still unlikely to trouble anyone who is not a specialist. In the nineteenth century the depth and structure of the novel changed, and here he has suffered from the realization that he never explored motive or character with any profundity. His followers in the historical novel are innumerable, and include Bulwer Lytton, Dickens, Thackeray, Reade, and George Eliot. Nor was his influence confined to England alone, for from France to Russia, and across the Atlantic to America, Scott was admired.

One novelist in this age stands apart from his contemporaries. Thomas Love Peacock (1785-1866) was a friend of Shelley, but a satirist of romanticism. He invented a novel which could contain irony, and conversation, and a mockery of romantic excesses. His characters exist as shadows only, but shadows with entertaining voices. His plots are only excuses for the voices to be heard exchanging the talk which Peacock had invented for them. Peacock himself had a wide learning, both classical and medieval, and in *Maid Marion* (1822) and the *Misfortunes of Elphin* (1829) he shows that he understands the attractions of romance. Few who have read his novels come away without entertainment, and *Headlong Hall* (1816), *Nightmare Abbey* (1818), *Crochet Castle* (1831), encouraged George Meredith and Aldous Huxley to try new ways in fiction.

CHAPTER ELEVEN

THE ENGLISH NOVEL FROM DICKENS TO THE PRESENT DAY

IN the nineteenth-century novel Charles Dickens (1812-70) is pre-eminent. In most ways he is the greatest novelist that England has yet produced. After his preliminary *Sketches by Boz* (1836), he published *Pickwick Papers* (1836-7), the supreme comic novel in our language. The comedy is never superimposed, for it is an effortless expression of a comic view of life. Dickens seems to see things differently, in an amusing and exaggerated way, and he plunges with much exuberance from one adventure to another, without any thought of plot or design. He is hampered by his age, which demands sentiment and reticence, but in the space that is allowed to him he scampers as if he knew no restraint. Had he the encouragement of a less squeamish age he would have been Shakespearian. Dickens enjoyed life, but hated the social system into which he had been born. There are many indications that he was halfway towards being a revolutionary, and in many of the later novels he was to attack the corruptions of his time. Yet his age exacted its penalty in demanding that his novels, if they were to be popular, should keep to the conventions of middle-class society in morality and in vocabulary. Never was he less embarrassed by restrictions than in the exuberance of *Pickwick Papers*. In *Oliver Twist*, which followed in 1838, pathos is beginning to intrude on humour, and Dickens, appalled by the cruelty of his time, is feeling that he must convey a message through fiction to his hard-hearted generation. His invention is still abundant, as he tells the story of the virtuous pauper boy who has to submit to perils and temptations. The strength lies less in the pathos than in the 'low' scenes, in the humour and satire of which the figure of Mr Bumble is the centre. With *Nicholas Nickleby* (1838-9) plot grows in importance, and Dickens shows his talent for the melodramatic. He draws his characters with the same firm lines as Ben Jonson had done in the seventeenth century. Satire is abundant in the Yorkshire school scenes, while much that is best lies in the humour of the theatre of Vincent Crummles and his company. *The Old Curiosity Shop* (1841) showed pathos transcendent over humour, especially in the death of little Nell: one feels that the only ritual known to Dickens's middle-class audience was the pageantry of funerals. *Barnaby Rudge* (1841), with its picture of the Gordon Riots, is Dickens's first attempt in the historical novel, and here plot, which had counted for nothing in *Pickwick Papers*, becomes increasingly important. Before *Martin Chuzzlewit* (1844) he made his American journey, and the American scenes in this novel gave offence. Yet all of Dickens is here: Pecksniff and his daughters, Sarah Gamp, Tom Pinch, the gentle, kindly Dickensian figure, Mark Tapley, vigorous and virtuous, a great variety of character and incident all well-managed. Between 1843 and 1848 he wrote his *Christmas Books*, including *The Christmas Carol*. The most popular perhaps of all his works, this shows his belief in human kindliness worked almost to mysticism. *Dombey and Son* in 1848 displayed by its increased control of pathos how much his art had developed since *The Old Curiosity Shop*. In *David Copperfield* (1850) he brought the first phase of his novel-writing to an end in a work with a strong autobiographical element, and with such firm characterization as Micawber and Uriah Heep.

Bleak House (1853) is the most conscious and deeply planned novel in Dickens's whole work, and clearly his art has moved far from the spontaneous gaiety of *Pickwick Papers*. It was followed by *Hard Times* (1854), a novel dedicated to Carlyle. While in all his work Dickens is attacking the social conditions of his time, here he gives this theme a special emphasis. He satirizes in Coketown and Mr Gradgrind the whole *laissez faire* system of the Manchester school and suggests that its enlightened self-interest is unenlightened cruelty. A social bias again governs *Little Dorrit* (1857), in which Dickens attacks the Circumlocution Office and the methods of bureaucracy: the picture of prison life, which was a comic motive in *Pickwick*

Papers, is now a serious theme in the portrayal of the debtors' prison. With *The Tale of Two Cities* (1859) he returned to the historical novel, and, inspired by Carlyle, laid his theme in the French Revolution. None of his works shows more clearly how wide and unexpected were the resources of his genius. He completed two other novels, *Great Expectations* (1861) and *Our Mutual Friend* (1864), before his premature death in 1870, and he left unfinished the manuscript of *The Mystery of Edwin Drood.*

Dickens had driven himself to death. From 1858 to 1868 he had given dramatic readings of his novels in England and America. They were profitable, and despite the weariness of the journeys, he delighted in the applause. An audience to Dickens was like a potent wine, and, to make sure of the potency, he had to please the audience. Shakespeare satisfied his audience, with no sacrifice of vision, but Dickens knew more than he revealed. His own nature was involved in a high emotionalism which prevented him from reaching the sense of tragedy of a Dostoievsky, or that full vision of life which makes Tolstoy supreme among the novelists of the world. Short of this he had everything. Like all great artists he saw the world as if it was an entirely fresh experience seen for the first time, and he had an extraordinary range of language, from comic invention to great eloquence. He invented character and situation with a range that had been unequalled since Shakespeare. So deeply did he affect his audiences that the view of life behind his novels has entered into our English tradition. Reason and theory he distrusted, but compassion and cheerfulness of heart he elevated into the supreme virtues. He knew in his more reflective moments that cheerfulness alone will not destroy the Coketowns of the world. This reflection he kept mainly to himself, and his intense emotionalism helped him to obscure it. When Dickens died in 1870 something had gone out of English life that was irreplaceable, a bright light that had shone upon the drab commercialism of the century, calling men back to laughter and kindliness, and the disruption of the cruelties in which they were entangling themselves.

William Makepeace Thackeray (1811-63) and Dickens were

such near contemporaries that it is natural that their work should have often been compared. In education and social status they were widely separated. Dickens had little regular education: his father was often in prison for debt and he himself had early started to earn his living in a blacking factory. Thackeray, born in Calcutta, the son of an East India Company official, had the benefits of Charterhouse and Cambridge. Dickens when he was poor knew the real meaning of poverty, but for Thackeray to be poor merely meant that for the time one relied on credit. Dickens was excitable, while Thackeray was lethargic and had to drive himself to composition.

Throughout his whole life Thackeray was a journalist. Up to 1854 he was a regular contributor to *Punch*, and later he was editor of *The Cornhill*. As a novelist he began late with *Vanity Fair* (1847-8) when he was thirty-six. Ten years later he was working at his last considerable novel, *The Virginians* (1857-9). For one brilliant decade the bright yellow shilling numbers, in which his novels were published, became a feature of English life. In those years he had published *Pendennis* (1848-50); *Henry Esmond* (1852); *The Newcomes* (1853-5). In 1863 he died. He was only fifty-two, and life seemed to have much to offer him. Only a year before he had built himself a mansion in Kensington. His tastes were extravagant and his income had to keep pace with them. Not for him the little house at £40 a year with 'a snuffy little Scotch maid to open the door' which seemed to suit Carlyle. Like Dickens he drove himself to give readings of his novels in London and in America. He flogged his income up to £10,000 a year, and this, and his methods of living, brought him down.

Vanity Fair showed him at his best, in a clear-sighted realism, a deep detestation of insincerity, and a broad and powerful development of narrative. His characterization and, indeed, all his effects are more subtle than in Dickens. He is less troubled by presenting a moral solution than by evoking an image of life as he has seen it. This gives the true mark of greatness to his portrait of Becky Sharp. She is an adventuress and a deceitful woman, but Thackeray so presents her that the audience can never retain an attitude of detached judgment.

As an artist he showed no consistent development from this first brilliant work. *Pendennis* and *The Newcomes* are too involved in digressions to have the strength of design which *Vanity Fair* possessed. The skill remains in individual scenes and characters. In the portrayal of sentiment he is more delicate than Dickens, and in Colonel Newcome he makes the final portrait of the ideal notion of an English gentleman. The defect in structure in these novels is corrected in *Henry Esmond,* in which Thackeray wrote an historical novel on the eighteenth century, a period of which his lectures on *The English Humorists* and *The Four Georges* show him a master. He reconstructed in *Esmond* the atmosphere of the age of Queen Anne, through a plot carefully devised, and with a theme difficult to control.

Though nothing in the early nineteenth century approaches Dickens and Thackeray, the novel in that period showed great variety. Fiction had become the dominant form in literature, and the problem of recording even its main types becomes difficult. Some novelists tried a number of different forms, as if they were attempting to adjust themselves to all the changes of public taste. Bulwer Lytton (1803-73) is an outstanding example of this versatility. Following Scott he produced a number of historical novels, of which *The Last Days of Pompeii* (1834) is the best known, and *Rienzi* (1835) possibly the most competent. He continued with a novel of terror, *Zanoni* (1844), and he made a popular union of the novel of crime and the novel of social protest in *Paul Clifford* (1830), and in *Eugene Aram* (1832), which had the added interest that it was based on recent events. Later, when the more realistic novel had re-established itself, he wrote *The Caxtons* (1849) and *My Novel* (1853). Bulwer Lytton's diversity has often led criticism to dismiss him too cursorily, as if he were merely a facile imitator. He has ingenuity and skill, and often a capacity for invention. His earliest novel, *Pelham* (1828), with its portrait of the Byronic rebel and dandy, is one of his most consistent works, while towards the close of his long career he wrote *The Coming Race* (1871), in which he anticipated the Utopian novel of Samuel Butler and H. G. Wells. There is a similar variety in the work of Charles Kingsley (1819-75), whose work varied from the propaganda novels of *Yeast* (1848) and *Alton Locke* (1850), advocating Christian Socialism, to historical romances such as *Hypatia* (1853) and *Westward Ho!* (1855), and the fantasy of *The Water Babies*. Variety the century did not lack, and much of the work cannot be easily defined: A. W. Kinglake (1809-91), who used the East as his background in *Eöthen* (1844); Sir Richard Burton, who translated *The Arabian Nights* (1885-8); and George Borrow, whose wanderings, adventures, and gipsy-lore are to be found in *Lavengro* (1851), *The Romany Rye* (1857), and *Wild Wales* (1862). The observation and alert vagrancy of Borrow recur again later in the century in Richard Jefferies (1848-87), in volumes such as *After London* (1885), and in W. H. Hudson (1846-1922) in his descriptions of South America and of rural England.

The social attack through the novel, which Dickens had exploited, was carried on with documentary exactness by Charles Reade (1814-84), as in his exposure of the prison system in his melodramatic narrative *It is Never too Late to Mend* (1856). Reade is sometimes compared to Zola, but this seems unfair to Zola, for though he had patience in the accumulation of facts, his exaggerated violence and pathos are only too often apparent. He was happier in his excursion into the historical novel in *The Cloister and the Hearth* (1861), where he portrays a lively and detailed, though largely illusory picture of the Middle Ages. A more powerful quality attaches to the novels of Benjamin Disraeli (1804-81), whose reputation as the most vital figure in the politics of the century has obscured him as a writer of fiction. His most effective work is to be found in the three novels which are an exposition of his political idealism: *Coningsby* (1844); *Sybil* (1845); and *Tancred* (1847). Here he advocated the 'Young England' policy of a Tory Democracy and his belief in a new conception of nationality. To re-read those novels is to find that neither in their themes nor in their politics are they as outworn as might be anticipated. In a very different way Mrs Gaskell (1810-65) exposed the cruelty of the industrial system as she had seen it in Manchester in *Mary Barton* (1848) and *North and South* (1855). She had a talent for combining social criticism and melodrama, though her skill is not confined to these novels of social protest, for in *Cranford* (1853) she showed gentleness and humour in a picture of provincial life. When Victorian readers wished to turn from politics or the social evils of their times, they had in Wilkie Collins (1824-89) a writer who could arouse mystery and terror in a far more subtle way than Horace Walpole or Mrs Radcliffe. In *The Woman in White* (1860) and *The Moonstone* (1868) he showed a poetical, almost a mystical quality in combination with the power for constructing an elaborate and well-defined mystery plot.

In originality none of these writers could compare with Charlotte and Emily Brontë. There is no story more inexplicable in our literature than the way in which these two sisters, living in the isolated village of Haworth, in Yorkshire, and with no encouragement from their domineering father, came to write novels which have been read with pleasure by successive generations of readers to this day. Their lives have often been recounted, but never more vividly than by Mrs Gaskell. Emily Brontë (1814-48) in her single novel *Wuthering Heights* (1847) created somehow out of her own imagination a stark, passionate world, reminiscent at times of the storm scenes in *King Lear*. In other hands the story might be mere melodrama, but so might *Othello* if told in a different way. As Emily Brontë narrates it, this story has a wild and cruel reality, and is original beyond any other novel in the century. How her mind came to conceive such a world can never be known, but behind her apparent loneliness there must have been a mysterious, ever-quickening inner activity, as her poems show. The talent of Charlotte Brontë (1816-55) was more diffuse but was maintained through a number of novels: *Jane Eyre* (1847); *Shirley* (1849); *Villette* (1853); and *The Professor* (1857). She combined scenes from her own life, in Yorkshire and in the school at Brussels, with the far richer and more romantic experiences which she had imagined. Thus her work is grounded in realism, but goes beyond into a wish-fulfilment. She had the courage to explore human life with greater fidelity than was common in her age, though the reticence of her period prevents her from following her themes to their logical conclusion. *Jane Eyre*, shows the elements that make up her conception of life. Jane was a governess, and part of the actuality of Charlotte's own life. But Jane, unlike Charlotte, goes to the house of Mr Rochester, with whom she is in love, and in Rochester she makes a figure of mystery, with a suggestion of the sinister. In part he is her fantasy of what the male as an instrument of sexual passion might be, and in part he is Montoni, or Byron transferred to a middle-class setting. The air of mystery which can be felt by the reader in every fibre of his being is created in Rochester's house. This was Charlotte Brontë's power, the creation of an atmosphere of terror without departing from a middle-class setting. For in few novels does the narrative make such a direct and physical impact. She lacked the courage to carry it farther into the wild, disordered world which Emily conceived in *Wuthering Heights*.

While the Brontës are still secure in their reputation, George Eliot's (Mary Ann Evans, 1819-80) has suffered something of a collapse though recent criticism has claimed for her a very high place among English novelists. Of all the women novelists of the nineteenth century, she was the most learned. Before she wrote fiction she had translated Strauss's *Leben Jesu*, and acted as assistant editor of the *Westminster Review*. She nearly married Herbert Spencer, the philosopher, only he found her too 'morbidly intellectual.' If Spencer could not marry her, he introduced her to G. H. Lewes, a writer of great competence. With Lewes she lived and he encouraged her to divert her attention from philosophy to fiction. Her early *Scenes of Clerical Life* (1857) had an immediate success. She followed these short narratives with a long novel, *Adam Bede* (1859), and her reputation was made. On the background of English rural life which she knew so well she created a far stronger theme than the Victorian novel previously permitted. In Hetty Sorrel she showed a young girl, seduced and led to child murder, and her imagination plays sympathetically around this lively and pathetic figure. While in Hetty she allowed a free play to her intuitions, her intellect controlled the 'good' characters in the novel, Dinah and Adam Bede. The problem for George Eliot as a novelist was whether her intuitions or her intellect would ultimately gain control.

In the end her intellect won, and that was the hour of her defeat as an artist. In *Adam Bede* she was still tolerably free, and in description and character she showed not only intimacy and understanding, but a power of humour, which in Mrs Poyser is reminiscent of Scott, or even Shakespeare. *The Mill on the Floss* (1860) showed her dilemma even more clearly. This was a Wordsworth story told in prose as a novel. In part, it is the life of a brother and sister, presented with great sensitiveness: the girl passionate, dimly mystical, introspective, reacting against the blunter and more boisterous values of the boy. All this George Eliot knew intuitively, but her intellect had constructed a plan for the novel which hardens this natural study into a melodramatic close. The different elements in her mind found a balance in the shorter narrative of *Silas Marner* (1861), where all is admirably ordered to one design. The turning-point of her career was her attempt in *Romola* (1863) to write an historical novel on the Italian Renaissance. All that learning could offer in preparation for the novel George Eliot possessed, but the spirit of that period of stangely conflicting values is absent, and Romola herself appears as some graceful nineteenth-century pre-Raphaelite who has wandered by mistake into Renaissance Italy. *Felix Holt* (1866), a novel of Radicalism of the Reform Bill period, with its over-elaborate plot, showed the penalties she was paying for the loss of her early spontaneity. But the end was not yet, for in *Middlemarch* (1871-2) she co-ordinated her powers to construct one of the great novels of the century. She has returned from the past to contemporary times, and gathers into sympathetic portraiture the lives of a number of families and studies their reactions. Her intellect seems to have been sufficiently employed in the different problem of structure not to impede her imagination. She had achieved the nearest approach in English to Balzac. In George Eliot's work, one is aware of her desire to enlarge the possibilities of the novel as a form of expression: she wishes to include new themes, to penetrate more deeply into character. Her contemporary, Anthony Trollope (1815-82), is dominated by no such ambitious desire. In his delightful *Autobiography* he discusses novel-writing as if it were as simple as cobbling. This modest attitude to his own art disguised for a time the appreciation of his pictures of clerical life, which began with *The Warden* (1855), and continued to *Barchester Towers* (1857). He had a very easy and quite unpretentious gift for narrative, a fertile imagination, a style that seems to carry the reader on effortlessly, and a happy imagination for creating character and incident. He is a male Jane Austen, cruder and more expansive, but equally secure in his knowledge of what he can do, and with the same clear determination not to transgress into worlds which he does not understand.

Trollope is the type of writer that is easily neglected by the historians of literature, for he made little contribution to the development of the novel. More original in structure and intention were his contemporaries George Meredith and Thomas Hardy. The reputation of George Meredith (1828-1909) has declined sadly in the middle decades of the twentieth century and attempts at a revival have met with only a modest response. That his novels are difficult must be admitted, but there was no more sensitive mind among the novel writers of the century. Intellectually his main weakness was a share of the pride which he condemned in his characters, and it may be admitted that he made the first chapters of his novels intentionally difficult, so that they might be sign-posts to the dull-witted to follow him no farther. Unfortunately, he has been neglected not by the dull-witted alone. For Meredith, the novel was far more than mere story-telling. Through his conception of comedy he wished to show up the dangers that beset the human spirit in its struggle to abandon the brutishness from which it had arisen. The body, the mind, and, above all, the heart betrayed men from the normality which constituted the ideal way of life. The heart was treacherous because of the excessive and insincere feelings which sentimentalism tempted it to affect. This teaching Meredith expounded in a series of incicents created to explore the 'finer' shades of sentiment. He is a nineteenth-century Richardson, with a much finer intelligence than Richardson possessed. Following this philosophical purpose, Meredith, in three of his novels, *Richard Feveril*, *Evan Harrington*, and *Harry Richmond*, analyses the most formative years in a young man's development, and the different types of entertainment provided by these three studies show how varied was his art. The study of sentimentalism led him later to give women characters a central position in his theme, and again the variety is maintained in such contrasting studies as *Rhoda Fleming* (1865), *Vittoria* (1867), and *Diana of the Crossways* (1885). At his best his work had the brilliance of a Restoration comedy, and this is suggested above all by *The Egoist* (1877). He had learned from his father-in-law, T. L. Peacock, how to use entertaining dialogue in the novel, but he is seldom content with brilliance alone. He is for ever dissecting the frailty and deceit of the human spirit. He seems at times to make life too complex, and as he progresses in his work the complexity increases until in *One of Our Conquerors* (1891), the reader may well feel that the effort demanded of him has not been fully rewarded.

Meredith's subtlety in the novel is paralleled in the work of Henry James (1843-1916), who, born and educated in America, settled in Europe in 1875 and was naturalized in 1915. His early novels, such as *Daisy Miller* (1879), portray the contact of Americans with European life. There followed a series of studies of English life itself, in *The Tragic Muse* (1890) and a number of other novels. As his work progressed, so did the intricacy of his style increase. He seemed to seek for every fine nuance of feeling and he discriminated with microscopic clarity, moods and changes that had not been previously apparent. This mature stage can be discovered in *The Wings of the Dove* (1902), *The Ambassadors* (1903), and particularly in *The Golden Bowl* (1904). Henry James belongs only in part to English literature. His view of Europe was only possible to one with his American background. He had longed for the imagined elegance of the Old World, its tradition, its courtesies, and its ritual. When he discovered that in reality they did not exist, he invented them, until his world is a Bostonian's platonic idea of what aristocratic life in Europe should be. With this idealization he combined a reticence in vocabulary, which arose not from any moral scruple but from a detestation of the vulgar and the physical. Sometimes in his work one longs for the spirit of Chaucer or Rabelais, or even for the blunt, clear *argot* of the street. He seems even to have hesitancy and faintheartedness in the whispered suggestions of his elaborate and insinuating sentences. Yet he had enlarged the conception of the novel itself by his subtle discriminations in sentiment, and by the presentation of human relationships. Here were the ruling classes of the old pre-war-world Europe, idealized, apotheosized, by one who had loved their culture so passionately that he could not see that life itself was far more cruel than his view would suggest. His strength as an artist lay in the consistency of this invented world, which was so faithfully recorded that often one could believe that it was not invented at all but only an elegant reality that one had missed.

If Henry James saw England as a stranger, Thomas Hardy (1840-1928) saw it as an Englishman born in Dorchester, and living for the greater part of his life in the Wessex which he portrayed. It is an interesting comment on the variety of the novelist's art that though Thomas Hardy and Henry James are contemporaries their worlds never meet. In 1871 Hardy published his first novel, *Desperate Remedies*, and from that year until the appearance of *Jude the Obscure* in 1895, he produced novels regularly, of which the most memorable by common consent are *The Return of the Native* (1878); *The Trumpet Major* (1880); *The Mayor of Casterbridge* (1886); *The Woodlanders* (1887); and *Tess of the D'Urbervilles* (1891). An architect by profession, he gave to his novels a design that was architectural, employing each circumstance in the narrative to one accumulated effect. The final impression was one of a malign Fate functioning in men's lives, corrupting their possibilities of happiness, and beckoning them towards tragedy. While this intuition about life did not harden into a philosophy, it was so persistent that it had every aspect of a doctrine. The intellect contributed to it in revolting against the optimism of nineteenth-century materialism, and in refusing the consolations of the Christian faith. While he saw life thus as cruel and purposeless, he does not remain a detached spectator. He has pity for the puppets of Destiny, and it is a compassion that extends from man to the earth-worms, and the diseased leaves on the trees. Such a conception gave his novels a high seriousness which few of his contemporaries possessed. It was as if a scene of Greek tragedy were being played out among his Wessex rustics. An early criticism of his work lay in this very incongruity, that his rustic characters should have the high passions, the noble and tragic proportions, which he gave them.

No theory can in itself make a novelist, and Hardy's novels, whether they are great or not, have appealed to successive generations of readers. He possessed varied gifts. First, he had supremely the gift of anecdote, the power of inventing lively incidents through which his story could move. He had patience in displaying through the incident the gradual interplay of his characters. His knowledge of country life made vivid the details in his stories, coloured and attractive in themselves, apart from their importance in the secure structure of his theme. Nor would he allow himself to be confined by the reticence which had limited the art of so many of his contemporaries. *Tess* and *Adam Bede* deal in part with the same theme, and to read them together is to see how far Hardy has progressed towards freedom of expression. In *Tess* and in *Jude the Obscure* he brought the novel in England near to the dignity of high tragedy. Nature, which to Wordsworth and the romantics had seemed stimulating and benign, appeared to Hardy as cruel and relentless. At the same time his kindliest characters are those who have lived away from the towns in a quiet rural life, refusing to challenge the wrathful spirits which play such havoc with life. His position as a novelist is difficult to assess with any certainty. At first he was condemned as a 'second-rate romantic' and in the year of his death he was elevated into one of the greatest figures of our literature. The first view is ill-informed and the second excessive, but the sincerity and courage and the successful patience of his art leave him a great figure in our fiction. In the European war of 1914-18 he was read with attention as one who had the courage to portray life with the grimness that it possessed and in portraying it not to lose pity. Often in times of stress Hardy's art will function in a similar way and so enter into the permanent tradition of our literature.

Both Meredith and Hardy had been influenced by the

teaching of Darwin and the biological scientists, and this influence is found in an even more open way in the work of Samuel Butler (1835-1902). In a century that was little given to satire he revived in *The Way of All Flesh* (1903) something of the spirit of Swift. This novel, which was largely autobiographical, showed an education in a clerical household, and in a bitter and comic manner destroyed the compromise with which Victorian society sheltered itself. In an even closer approach to Swift's manner Butler attacked contemporary values in two satires, *Erewhon* (1872) and *Erewhon Revisited* (1901). Intellectually he was a rebel, and while this drove him at times into eccentricity, it allowed him to challenge all the values upon which society was basing itself. Butler saw that the worship of the machine made man its slave and that the machine as master would challenge and destroy civilization. He explores the treatment of disease, crime, and education, exposing the shallow inconsistencies and dubious values on which the confident action of society is based. He does not approach as closely as Swift to despair, for one is aware ever of a certain zest and enjoyment in life. He has also a quiet, wan optimism. If reason were allowed to function, he believes that life might be tolerable and kindly. Much that Butler wrote reads today like prophecy, and in his essays as well as his fiction he shows himself one of the most original minds of his time. His contribution was rather to ideas than to the form of fiction, though the opening of *Erewhon* shows how naturally and vividly he could write.

Between 1870 and 1880 there appear new values both in the fiction produced and in the audience which reads it. There is an increase in the number of people who can read, and many of them are without tradition and opposed to the long three-volume novels which have previously been popular. Publishers did not at once become aware of this change, but gradually they found that shorter and cheaper volumes were more profitable. Robert Louis Stevenson (1850-94) was one of the earliest writers to make publishers aware of these changes. He had published without much success, in a boys' periodical, a romance entitled *Treasure Island.* When an enterprising publisher reissued this in volume form it was immediately popular with the new adult public. With the short novel came the short story, to which Edgar Allan Poe had already given such vogue in America. Stevenson again made an important contribution, with the *New Arabian Nights* (1882). There followed a number of romances and mystery stories, including *Kidnapped* (1886), *The Black Arrow* (1888), *The Master of Ballantrae* (1889), and *The Wrong Box* (1889). In *Dr Jekyll and Mr Hyde* he departed from his usual manner to write a modern allegory of the good and evil in the human personality. At his death he was working on an unfinished novel, *Weir of Hermiston*, which some have thought the most finished product of his whole work. Stevenson in all that he wrote, in his essays, his letters, and his novels, remained an artist. He was in style self-conscious, exacting from himself perfection. Sometimes, indeed, one is led to think that the style was too good for the work. Stevenson is leading the novel back towards story-telling and to the romance. It could be led to worse places, but one is conscious of the difference between him and the great masters of the art.

Stevenson is so consistent an artist that it is difficult at first to realize the phenomenon that had produced his success. The new reading public wanted a fiction that was easy, and not too long. This type of demand had always been present, but with the increase in the reading public, the clamour for it increased. From this time onwards one can detect two types of fiction-writers: those who deliberately or naturally adapt themselves to the great public, and those who follow their art into more difficult places and are often denied popular esteem. Thus the history of the great successes from 1870 is not necessarily the basis of the history of English fiction in that period. The following, for instance, is a list of the writers who in their day have been outstandingly successful: 'Ouida,' Rider Haggard, Conan Doyle, Mrs Humphry Ward, Hall Caine, Marie Corelli, Grant Allen, and Edgar Wallace. All of their work was simple enough for the great audience to understand, though their approach to fiction as an art varied. Most of them could tell a story, and this is particularly true of such writers as Conan

Doyle in the Sherlock Holmes stories, or even Edgar Wallace, who, had he taken more pains, might have written work that mattered. Rider Haggard again misses only by a little the opportunity of being something more than a writer of successful romances. He is obviously so much more competent than Grant Allen, whose *The Woman Who Did* was in 1895 not only topical, but daring. It was also a topical element that swept Mrs Humphry Ward's *Robert Elsmere* into every drawing-room in England. Her popularity was due not to the new, uneducated audience, but to the fact that in her discussions of the Christian faith she seized upon a theme uppermost in the mind of her time. Sometimes popularity may disguise an author's genuine merit. So P. G. Wodehouse's reception by a vast audience has obscured the fact that he is not only a writer of most brilliant idiomatic English but that he has added to our vocabulary. It is dangerous to judge any writer solely in the terms of the reception that he receives. At the same time, from the eighties onwards the production of a large amount of very competent fiction written solely with the eye on the audience complicates any account of the novel at the present time.

The problem can be seen in some of its difficulties in the reception given to two writers, both of great merit, George Gissing and Rudyard Kipling. George Gissing (1857-1903) has never been a popular writer and is never likely to be. Yet no one in English fiction faced the disease of his century with such a frank realism. In *Workers in the Dawn* (1880), *Demos* (1886), *The Nether World* (1889), *New Grub Street* (1891), he portrayed the corruption of society and refused to his audience the promise of an easy solution. It may be that this sense of helplessness has made him unpopular with the Englsih who prefer an element of comedy in their tragedy, and accept the grim pages of a Dickens if only they are accompanied by sufficient material for laughter. A kindlier atmosphere plays around *The Private Papers of Henry Ryecroft* (1903), and possibly this has made that genial volume the most popular of his works. Rudyard Kipling (1865-1936), on the other hand, gained great popularity because his art naturally expressed much that a wide audience in England wished to hear. His work appeared at a time when England was becoming increasingly conscious of her Imperial position, and Kipling, born in India and still living there, was able to give the colour and the strangeness of the greatest country which Englishmen in their adventures overseas had encountered. Like Stevenson he was a master both of the short story and the short novel, and this brevity, again, helped to attach him easily to the taste of his day.

Beginning with *Plain Tales from the Hills* (1888), he continued with volumes of short stories and with novels that included *The Light that Failed* (1891) and *Kim* (1901). Though the Indian scene was the source of his first popularity, he also wrote an original story of school life, *Stalky and Co.* (1899); the well-known animal stories of *The Jungle Books* (1894 and 1895), and the Sussex, fairy-world theme of *Puck of Pook's Hill* (1906). In India he had all the advantage of a new background, and his own style, quick and pungent, captured its strange sights and colours. He saw the East, romantically it is true, as part of the White Man's Burden, but his conviction was sufficiently strong to give force to his presentation. Nor were his Englishmen in India all alike; he could play maliciously with the social life of Simla while he presented, with approval, the soldiers, and all who did a day's work efficiently. This delight in efficiency gave him pleasure in the mechanical aspects of his age, and often his imagery is derived from mechanism. His style was as simple in form as that of the Bible, but he had a lively imagination which threw in the vivid but unexpected word to enliven the sentence. So certain was he in his narrative that each period seems to be inevitable and nothing is wasted. Seldom does he attempt to present subtle characters, but in a few firm strokes he places his people into the narratives which he could tell so well.

Kipling was the voice of Imperialism triumphant, though there were signs, particularly in his poem *Recessional*, that he knew the dangers into which England might be led. Self-criticism, and even self-condemnation, appeared in the novel of the early twentieth century to an extent which Kipling would not have approved. With such a mood did John Galsworthy (1867-1933) begin his career as a novelist with *The*

Island Pharisees (1904). Later, in a series of volumes beginning with *The Man of Property*, he portrayed the life of the contemporary upper-middle classes. Published as *The Forsyte Saga* this series, and its sequels, had great popularity in England and on the Continent. After his death his reputation suddenly declined, so that today it is difficult to say what his final position will be. At his best he has a gift similar to that of Anthony Trollope of making a whole class in society come to life. But he departs from Trollope in attempting through this portraiture to assess the values of his age. To do this he has imposed a simple formula upon his action. In *The Forsyte Saga* this is defined as the struggle of Beauty against the Idea of Property or Possession. Irene is Beauty and Soames Forsyte, her husband, is the Idea of Possession, exacting, even forcibly, his marital rights from her. The weaker part of Galsworthy's art lay in this desire to take sides, for while his intellect started with a firm desire to satirize the Forsytes, some deeper intuition led him to sympathize with Soames, until in the later novels the author and his villain are in an almost sentimental relationship. This obscurity in his own vision has angered the younger readers of his work, but it need not lead them to underestimate his talent. In the firm, broad portrayal of half a century of English life as it appeared to the upper-middle classes Galsworthy has no equal.

While Galsworthy portrayed the upper-middle classes, Arnold Bennett (1867-1931) showed the life of the 'Five Towns,' the 'Potteries' of Staffordshire, and of the men and women who went out from them to see the world. He is an artist who too often succumbed to the temptations which a commercial world offers to the successful. In *The Card* he described the character who 'wheedled' his way to success and enjoyed the fashionable hotels and the showy elegance of the capital. Bennett was a literary 'Card,' and much of his work was written solely to provide for himself a luxurious atmosphere which should be as unlike the 'Five Towns' as possible. But if he was sometimes a 'Card' he was often an artist, and *The Old Wives' Tale* (1908) is as satisfactory a novel as was written in the period. He had learned in that work from European models, particularly from Maupassant, and his firm portrayal of two sisters of contrasting personality has a complete integrity. With this may be placed his rather more ponderous trilogy *Clayhanger* (1910), *Hilda Lessways* (1911), and *These Twain* (1916). Bennett is undisturbed by the desire to impart a message, which infected Galsworthy's art. He has a genuine naturalism accompanied by a useful gift for comedy.

Across the whole field of fiction of the twentieth century are scattered the innumerable publications of H. G. Wells (1868-1946). From the time when he jumped the counter of the draper's stores, where he was apprenticed, until his death over sixty years later, Wells continued to write novels, essays, histories, outlines, and programmes for world regeneration. He is the Rousseau of our age, and, whatever posterity may have to say of him, there are few educated Englishmen of two generations who have not owed something to his lively intelligence. He was the new education active in fiction: the pupil-teacher and the student in Huxley's biological lectures, disclosing his new knowledge to the world. Fiction, though only one of his modes of expression, has been the form to which he has been most consistently attached. He began in *The Time Machine* (1895) to employ his scientific imagination to invent a new form of scientific romance. His knowledge gave an authenticity to his narratives, and his ingenious use of detail added to their attraction. So, in quick succession, appeared *The Invisible Man* (1897); *The War of the Worlds* (1898); *When the Sleeper Wakes* (1899); and *The First Men in the Moon* (1901). These early romances accepted the world without much criticism, and delighted solely in working out an invention with some regard for scientific possibility. But in the romances which followed, *The Food of the Gods* (1904) and *In the Days of the Comet* (1906) ideas began to intrude. Wells was already a Socialist, though always one of his own definition, and he wished to bring some of the precision of science, and the order of the laboratory, into human life. In 1905 there followed *A Modern Utopia*, where, with some help from Plato, he portrayed a vision of a reasonable world. Fortunately, added to this interest in ideas he had a gift for comedy which was almost Dickensian. This he exploited in three joyous novels which must always stand high in his achievement: *The Wheels of Chance* (1896); *Love and Mr Lewisham* (1900); and, best of all, *Kipps* (1906). There followed a period when he attempted to attach his power for portraying living types to the presentation of contemporary problems. Wells had always asserted that he was a journalist rather than an artist, and that he was content if a novel could be a portmanteau for ideas. Though in this estimate he is less than just to himself, the mark of the period lies heavily upon *Ann Veronica* (1909), his portrait of the emancipated woman, and *The New Machiavelli* (1911), which interpreted a number of political movements of the time. In *Tono Bungay* (1909), however, he mastered this new form and exposed the evils of commercial publicity in a novel rich in enduring comedy. Nor did he forget the earlier joyous manner of *Kipps*, to which he returned in *The History of Mr Polly* (1910). During the European war he turned from fiction to write, without adequate preparation, on religion; but in one novel, *Mr Britling Sees it Through* (1916), he recorded, as no one else had done, the reactions of a sensitive mind to that war. During those years his thought became increasingly occupied with the problem of the New Europe, which all men of good faith hoped at that time would develop. His later work often diverted from fiction in an attempt to make his contribution to this reorganization. He saw that the modern world to be reasonable must be organized as a single unit, and he attempted to interpret the past of the world in *The Outline of History* (1920), so that the future might be more securely built. He had continued with fiction in this latter period, but, despite some experiments, it is fair on the whole to say that he made his novels increasingly the vehicle of his ideas. Sometimes, as in *The World of William Clissold* (1926), he seems to be disguising a series of essays with the form of a novel. No one can well understand the twentieth century, in its hopes and its disillusionments, without studying Wells. Uneven as his work is, the danger is to underestimate him. He had been able to transfer whole cross-sections of English life into the novel, and in the earlier romances to throw vivid fantasies upon the future. He had a style which was never pretentious but very plastic, and his rich humour coloured his novels, except in the later period when, as in *Joan and Peter* (1918), he fell into a steady treatise on education. The most enduring things in his work, apart from the earlier romances, will probably be *Kipps* and *Tono Bungay*, for he was at his best when the spirit of Dickens walked in company with his own enquiring mind.

Apart from the social novelists, the practice of fiction in the early twentieth century showed great variety, and some of the authors who began then are still alive and their work uncompleted. By common consent one of the most original of them was Jozef Korzeniowski, a Pole, born in the Ukraine, a captain in the English merchant marine, and ultimately a naturalized British citizen known to English readers as Joseph Conrad (1856-1924). With a wide experience of the sea and of Asia and the Americas and the ports of the world, he wrote, in an English that was elaborate and strangely rhythmical, a series of novels beginning with *Almayer's Folly* (1895), and including *The Nigger of the Narcissus* (1898); *Youth* (1902); *Typhoon* (1903); *Nostromo* (1904); *Lord Jim* (1906), and many others, to *The Arrow of Gold* (1919). The basis for Conrad's fiction is the adventure story, but it is told with a complex evocation of mood and a constant psychological interest in character. It is as if the work of R. L. Stevenson had been re-written by Henry James. He is self-conscious in his art, and the self-consciousness intrudes. He seeks like Flaubert for perfection, and sometimes the reader may watch him making his slow progress to his ideal. Often he writes of violence and danger, but not of these alone, for, like some of the 'impressionist' painters, he seeks to capture elusive moods, using a rich and coloured vocabulary, almost as if he employed words like pigments. While the surface reactions of life are in his novels, he seeks, as do some of the Russian novelists, for the more mysterious moods of consciousness. He has a greater integrity as an artist than many of his age, and one forgets that he is a foreigner writing English as one follows the strange and complex beauty of his prose.

Joseph Conrad helped to give a cosmopolitan variety to the novel by his very origins, and much of the enterprise in the fiction of the twentieth century has come from an interest in foreign models. So George Moore (1852-1933) profited by his years in France with a study of Zola, Maupassant, and the Goncourts. His work is difficult to judge, for he has been surrounded by ardent admirers who feel that any gesture of criticism is a mixture of heresy and vulgarity. He was self-consciously an artist but he was also a poseur, and his prose though often beautiful is seldom free from affectation. Irish by birth but Parisian by education, he dramatized his conception of himself as an artist, and possibly his best work is to be found not in the novels but in a series of autobiographical narratives, including *Confessions of a Young Man* (1888); *Hail and Farewell: Ave* (1911), *Salve* (1912), *Vale* (1914). It must be admitted that this summary depresses him far below the place often allowed him. His talent was varied, and included the bold naturalism of *Esther Waters* (1894), and the graceful and refined prose of *The Brook Kerith* (1916), a religious novel, and *Héloïse and Abélard* (1921).

Popularity sometimes affects the judgments of critics in estimating the worth of a writer, and no modern author has suffered in this way as much as W. Somerset Maugham (*b.* 1874). His early novels, which included *Liza of Lambeth* (1897), were realist studies of London life, but in his later novels he has used China and Malaya as his background in *The Trembling Leaf* (1921), and *The Painted Veil* (1925). These, and a number of other novels and volumes of short stories, should have established him as a writer of importance, but criticism has often neglected him. His early studies in Maupassant gave him an admirable economy in narrative, while his attachment to French literature helped him to exclude sentimentality from his work and to deal with sexual relations with an unabashed frankness which English readers find disconcerting. He conveys no message, as do so many of his contemporaries, and when life appears in unpleasant patterns he records them without apology. His realism has often been mistaken for cynicism, but it is well to remember that in his prose he has the unaffected strength of Swift; and that something of Swift's vision, without Swift's disgust at life, can be found in his work.

While Maugham may have suffered from being too popular, the work of E. M. Forster (*b.* 1879) has not had, except in limited circles, the encouragement that it deserves, though some would name him as one of the greatest English novelists of the century. He has written sparingly. Enlightened judgments found his *Howard's End* (1911) one of the most illuminating novels of the years immediately before the war of 1914-18, but it was long before he was to gain any wide recognition, which came with *A Passage to India* (1924). This novel is an admirable corrective to Kipling's work, for with a realism that is subtly evoked Forster shows, not the romance of the East, but the actual types, and with a minimum of description he creates the atmosphere in which they lived. The governing mood of *A Passage to India* is satirical, and the same spirit was to be found in a number of writers of the time, including the ironical mysticism of T. F. Powys's *Mr Weston's Good Wine* (1928), and the more obvious intentions of Miss Rose Macaulay in *Orphan Island* (1924), and in similar narratives.

Of the novelists who have gained great popularity in the last decades it is still difficult to write. That they have brought far greater intelligence and skill than their predecessors may easily be allowed, without attempting any final determination of their place in the history of the novel as a whole. It must always be remembered that the modern world of letters is divided into sects, and to the Brahmins to be popular is to be condemned. Without attempting to name all the writers of this category two may be taken as examples, Sir Hugh Walpole (1884-1941), and J. B. Priestley (*b.* 1894). Sir Hugh Walpole began as a writer of fiction in 1910 with *The Wooden Horse*, and he published consistently from that date. His studies of varied types of English life, sometimes reminiscent of Trollope, as in *The Cathedral* (1922), were filled with an idealism which yet did not ignore the cruel and the sinister in life. More recently he concluded a long historical novel, *Rogue Herries* (1930). In all that long work he never fell below a certain standard which he set for himself, and though it has its obvious limitations it allowed him to penetrate into many aspects of experience.

Posterity may judge! J. B. Priestley's meteoric rise with *The Good Companions* (1929) has been followed by *Angel Pavement* (1930) and other novels. Those who dislike popularity have vehemently attempted to minimize his achievement. Beginning with his Yorkshire background, he has, in his expansive volumes, been able to elucidate much in the contemporary scene. He has appealed to a vast audience that was not aware of fiction before it encountered his work, the audience that Dickens captured. Some love for his fellow-men, and a love for England, endows his portraiture with part of his liveliness. He has given large and widespread pleasure to his generation, and the next generation, when it comes, alone will know whether that pleasure is to continue.

While these writers achieve their own purposes without modifying the form of fiction, a number of contemporary novelists have attempted to expand the novel as a medium of expression. The most vital, in many ways, was D. H. Lawrence (1885-1930), the son of a miner in a village near Nottingham, whose tormented life is well recorded in his *Letters*. His background was different from that of any novelist of his time. He knew the miners, their wives, the cramped houses, the huddled life, the cruelties and debasements and the smell of the slag heaps. But he knew, too, the country near-by, and sometimes he seems to ache for its fresh smells, its signs of growth, the sounds of birds, and the foot-prints of a fox in the snow. If the background was different, so was the inner experience. Modern civilization, as he had seen it, thwarted his spirit and he could find no consolation, as H. G. Wells had done, in making blue-prints for a new world. The disease was one which admitted no intellectual cure, for the modern world seemed to Lawrence to have corrupted man's emotional life. Even passion had become some niggling by-product of the intelligence. To discover again a free flow of the passionate life became for him almost a mystical ideal, for there was fulfilment and there was power. His early novels, of which the most successful was *Sons and Lovers* (1913), had only hinted at these later developments. He had been content in this, the most normal of his works, with a vivid, realistic picture of the

Nottingham life which he knew. Gradually his own philosophy asserted itself in his fiction, in *The Rainbow* (1915), *Women in Love* (1921), *Aaron's Rod* (1922). The European war, in which for medical reasons he had been a non-combatant, increased his sense of isolation, as he showed in *Kangaroo* (1923), the most revealing if not the most satisfactory of his works. This detachment from civilized life now became mixed with a certain irritability accompanied by a sense of surrender, and as he shows in *The Plumed Serpent* (1926) he sought among more primitive people in Mexico for the more natural life which Europe could not give. In its emphasis on the physical his work had aroused criticism in some quarters, and some of his novels had been banned. As if in revenge, he published in *Lady Chatterley's Lover* (1928) a franker description of the physical relations of two lovers than had yet appeared in English fiction. Though he wrote with great care he added nothing to the form of the novel, though his own philosophy led to a much bolder description of sexual life than his predecessors had given. Much in his work may be condemned. He rejected tradition, partly because he had never known it, and instead of struggling to remake civilization he turned upon it a loathing that culminated in despair. The intellect, one of the major instruments allowed to man if he is to seek the reasonable life, he despised. So much may be said on the adverse side of the balance, and it must be admitted that in these directions his influence has been pernicious. But it is difficult to judge in a cold and calculating way one who suffered so much. Nor even in the most detached summary can the estimate be left in this negative condition. His plea, taken in its simplest forms, that civilization had degraded man's sexual life, was a pertinent one. At one period his belief in the passions seems almost to become mystical, as if he were regaining something of Blake's vision. But his sense of isolation thwarted him, and at length almost degraded his genius. To style, in the ordinary definition of the word, he was indifferent. He seems to hack his meaning out of the words, as his forebears had hacked coal from the pits. But the effects are original. He invented a language in which sexual experience can be described, and he had a rare eye for every movement in nature, as if there, without knowing it, he found the sole consolation for his spirit.

The boldness of expression which D. H. Lawrence had brought into the novel was found also in his younger contemporary, Aldous Huxley (*b.* 1894). No finer intelligence has applied itself to fiction in this century, and though for a time he submitted to Lawrence's influence, no man could have had such a different background. In him the great influences of Victorian art and science met: on his father's side he was descended from Thomas Huxley, who had been Charles Darwin's champion in the discussions on evolution, and, on his mother's side, from Matthew Arnold. His education was not that of the Nottingham mining village, but of Eton and Balliol. Heredity with Huxley seems to have counted more than formal education, for he brought to the novel the knowledge and analysis of a scientist, and the curiosity in form of an artist. No writer images more clearly the changing temperament of intellectual England in the decades since the European war of 1914-18. His early novels, where one can sometimes detect the influence of Peacock, were comic and satiric narratives, prefiguring the complete disillusionment of young Englishmen in the years after the World War. In *Crome Yellow* (1921), and *Antic Hay* (1923), he seems to revel in the comic exposure of the deceit of life. Gradually—and here he is a little in advance of his generation—the cynicism gives place to more serious enquiry and results in *Those Barren Leaves* (1925). He is not seeking any easy solution of his dilemma, for like Lawrence he is tormented by the strange phenomenon of man, the animal who has a mind. Unlike Lawrence, he cannot regard sexual experience with any sense of pleasure, and certainly not as a medium of illumination. The theme fascinates him, but at the same time fills him with disgust. He watches the petty lecheries of his characters, unable to detach himself, and yet tortured almost by his preoccupation. Like Swift, he is angered at the jest that makes life thus, but, unlike Swift, he is aware that this strange beast, man, has also created symphonies, painted pictures, and had moments of vision. These preoccupations lead to the most brilliant and original of his novels. *Point Counter Point* (1928). In the brittle illusion of a well-ordered mechanical world, such as H. G. Wells would prescribe, he can find no consolation, and more deeply under Lawrence's influence than elsewhere, he satirizes such beliefs in *Brave New World* (1932). From 1933 the changed political scene in Europe has given to his thought a greater urgency and an enhanced seriousness. The beast, which he had already discovered in man, now seems rampant and ready to destroy the graces which had offered to the civilized world at least a minor compensation. In *Eyeless in Gaza* (1936) he expounds this deepened vision, and original though the volume is in form one feels that he has reached a certain impatience with fiction as a medium. The philosopher has overcome the artist, and the teacher has exorcized the cynic. So he is led in *Ends and Means* (1937) to set out his ideas without the embarrassment of a story, and he leaves fiction, though obviously only for a while. In his more recent work, written mainly in California, he has returned at times to fiction, and once, and very successfully to drama in *The Gioconda Smile*, but his Main preoccupation has continued with philosophy in an attempt to reconcile the East and the West.

While the novel in Lawrence and Huxley depends mainly on ideas, a group of writers in the present century have employed it to explore the inner aspects of the human personality. Some of them have been encouraged by the study of the subconscious to penetrate beneath the surface reactions in life. They believe that the novelist who portrays a mind as if it conducted its thought in well-ordered sentences is giving only an artificial impression. This portrayal of the inner life has often entered into the novel, but in the present age it has been explored more profoundly, with the aid of the psychological sciences, which have shown how disordered is our hidden mental existence. One of the earliest novelists of this type in England was Dorothy Richardson, whose *Pointed Roofs* (1915) is the first instalment of a series of novels in which the consciousness of a single character was exposed. Her work has not received the recognition accorded to Mrs Virginia Woolf, who began in the same year as Dorothy Richardson with *The Voyage Out* (1915), and who developed her art in a number of novels which include *Night and Day* (1919); *Jacob's Room* (1922); *Mrs Dalloway* (1925); *To the Lighthouse* (1927); *Orlando* (1928); *The Waves* (1931); and *The Years* (1937). Her tragic death by suicide in 1941 seemed to mark the end of a period. For she belonged to a privileged, generous, and highly cultured Liberalism whose opportunities seemed exhausted. Her method is usually to accept a plot which has a simple outline, but to exploit it with an impressionism which seizes upon every detail, however minute, and to order these details not in a rational arrangement but as they stream through the mind of one of her characters. The novel is thus becoming an interior soliloquy, though diffuseness is avoided by the retention of the central and well-ordered theme. She was armed with an acute intelligence which made this perception of every evanescent mood possible, while a diffused romantic quality added to the buoyancy of the narration. Wit accompanied her intelligence, as can be seen most obviously in *Orlando*, and a tenderness without sentimentality aided her in evoking these previously unapprehended human relations. The characters which she thus captures in the undress of their mental life are such as share her intelligence and her decencies. Even if she appears to have exposed all, there is much still to disclose. One may not be aware of it as one reads her novels, but one can see it once her work is compared with that of James Joyce

James Joyce (1882-1941) is for better or for worse the most original novelist of the century. His early short stories, *The Dubliners*, were brief impressionistic studies, as clear-cut as the stories of Maupassant. His individual art began to show itself in *A Portrait of the Artist as a Young Man* (1916), and appeared fully formed in *Ulysses* (1922). After seventeen years this was followed by *Finnegans Wake* (1939). Joyce attempts to make fiction that shall image the whole of life, conscious and subconscious, without any concessions to the ordinary conventions of speech. He would break up the ordinary structure of the language until it can image these fluctuating impressions. More philosophically, he comes to feel that time and space are artificial, and that all is related, and that art should be a symbol of that relationship. His work has become notorious, because in this pursuit he described, particularly in the close of *Ulysses*, these inner contemplations of his characters when they concentrate on their own sexual life. To judge him from these passages alone is to miss his seriousness as an artist. He had Dublin and the Catholic Church as his background, and from them both he revolted, as can be seen in *The Portrait of the Artist*. Both were highly organized unities, and to leave them, particularly to leave the Church, was emotionally to enter into Chaos. Psychologically Joyce is for ever attempting to re-seek unity in a world that is disorganized. The greater his attempt to define the Unity, the more do the broken fragments fall in minute pieces through his hands. Compared with *Finnegans Wake*, the outline of *Ulysses* is simple. Instead of the wanderings of Homer's Ulysses over the geographical world, Joyce shows the mental wanderings of a character in Dublin for the space of twenty-four hours. He retains sometimes the ordinary grammatical structure in the sentences, and the sequences of thought, once one has caught his devices for suggesting the free association in the mind, are not difficult to follow. By the side of *Finnegans Wake* the earlier novel seems a primer, for in this immense work Joyce has written a collection of words, some derived from language other than English, and many apparently invented, whose significance no single reader can ever hope to gain. His genius is, however, a sincere one and his boldness in invention has influenced a number of younger writers who have followed him at a modest distance.

One has to take leave of the English novel in a work which is incomprehensible, and it may be that in the future some writers will come back to simpler methods. For as it was suggested at the beginning, the novel is a story told in a special way. With Joyce there is a danger that 'the special way' has overlaid the story altogether. Without the story fiction cannot live, and one thing is certain that somehow the story will re-assert itself.

CHAPTER TWELVE

ENGLISH PROSE TO THE EIGHTEENTH CENTURY

WHEN life is the criterion and not art, the prose of a nation is far more important than its poetry. Into prose go its laws and proclamations, its prayers, and its politics, and, in modern times at least, its philosophy and history. The best that a nation can ask of its law-givers, politicians, and philosophers is a prose that is unpretentious, unambiguous, and unadorned. Apart from all this, the artist employs prose in a number of ways, in fiction, in the essay, and in drama. Often he wishes to use prose with elaborate patterns and richly decorative words. The artist may also use a simple prose, but with him the simplicity will be accompanied by power and eloquence. Rhetoric and the quest for harmony will always be beckoning him away from simplicity to more elaborate effects. Any study of prose is complicated by the very varied purposes for which prose is used. In this chapter the novel and the drama are eliminated, for they have already been considered, and an attempt is made, not to record the work of all the other important writers who have employed prose, but only of such as have added to the possibilities of English prose as a medium of expression.

Behind English prose, from the Anglo-Saxon period to the eighteenth century, is the pattern of Latin. Boethius's *Consolation of Philosophy*, a Latin work of the sixth century, was translated by King Alfred (*d.* 901), by Chaucer (*d.* 1400), and by Queen Elizabeth (*d.* 1603). A single Latin work had retained such distinguished popularity for over seven hundred years. Throughout that period most educated people could speak and write Latin, and some of them regarded Latin as the language in which all literature should be written. Even as late as the seventeenth century, Francis Bacon was afraid that English would 'play bankrupt' with authors, and determined that all he valued most in his work should exist in a Latin version. In

English there has been continuously an ambitious prose, usually with the memory of Latin behind it, and another, simpler prose, which approaches the ordinary native speech rhythms.

Early pre-Conquest literature had both kinds of prose; Aelfric wrote a prose that was consciously mannered, while the compilers of King Alfred's *Chronicle* wrote simply. The simple prose lives on much better than the mannered prose, and in movement it is like modern prose. Much of it is a bare and direct record of fact, but when the chronicler has to express an emotion he does so with a sincerity which is still intelligible. W. P. Ker translates a passage made by a Peterborough monk describing the misfortunes of the reign of Stephen as one of the most effective:

'Was never yet more wretchedness in the land, nor did the heathen men worse than these men did. For never anywhere did they spare either church, or churchyard, but took all the wealth therein, and afterwards burned the church and all together.'

Although the *Chronicle* began under Alfred's guidance, it continued for two and a half centuries after his death, and for almost a century after the Norman Conquest. It is sometimes suggested that English prose died out with the Conquest, but this is not true. What did die was the elaborate and mannered prose, such as that of Aelfric. What lived on was the simple, natural prose, such as the monk at Peterborough continued to write to 1154. There is thus a continuous tradition in English prose, though after the Conquest English is for a time debased, and has to struggle for existence. So in these centuries, when French is the fashionable language and the official language, English is still used, though the works in which it was employed were unexciting. Verse was employed in stories and romances, and prose had to carry the duller burdens of moral instruction, education, and history. But the homely, secure effects, found in the pre-Conquest prose, were not forgotten. It was not long after the *Chronicle* had ceased that English was used, in the thirteenth century, for the prose lives of St Margaret, St Katharine, and St Juliana, and in the *Ancren Riwle*, a book of instruction for nuns. This last, which combines moralizing and some mysticism with practical instruction and genuine human feeling, is a work few may now wish to read, but it remains as a proof of our long prose tradition.

The proof of the continuance of this tradition in the early fifteenth century is more ample, though the demonstration is again from works such as Reginald Pecock's *The Repressor* (1455), which no modern reader is likely to read except with some ulterior motive. The most important event in fifteenth-century prose was the establishment by William Caxton of his printing press in England in 1476. Caxton was not only a printer but a translator, and much concerned with the problem of extending the vocabulary of English. His own influence, and still more that of the printing press, helped to break down the anarchy of dialects and to give England a standard language.

Among the works which Caxton printed was Sir Thomas Malory's *Morte D'Arthur* (written about 1470). Composed in a prose intelligible to any modern reader, the words in Malory's sentences have a beauty of movement which cannot escape unnoticed. Malory's work was a translation of a number of French stories and was not conceived as a unity. Through it the chivalry and romance of the Middle Ages were recorded by a mysterious figure much of whose life was marked by violence and crime. As a complement, Lord Berners, in his translation of Froissart's *Chronicles* (1520), gave the realistic life of the same period. Froissart had narrated the life of the fourteenth century as he had seen it, and his vividness and honesty have made him a great descriptive historian. Berners allows Froissart's French to guide him into an English which is firm, intelligible, and simple. The range of the narrative is wider than in Malory, and the matter less archaic. In some ways, with Berners' translation of Froissart modern prose in England may be said to have begun. Meanwhile, the Bible, which had been appearing in various forms in the vernacular, was approaching the translation in which it was to become for centuries the best-known book in English. The English Bible as it is known today owes its form mainly to the labours of two men, William Tyndale (1490-1536) and Miles Coverdale (1488-1568). Already in the fourteenth century John Wycliffe (1324-84) had laboured to make an English version, but his renderings were based on the Vulgate, or Latin version, and his English was literal and stiff. His influence on the development of English prose has been exaggerated. Tyndale, who at Vilvorde in 1536 was strangled at the stake for heresy, and his body burnt, gave to his prose the simple vigour of phrase, and the strong cadences, with which the Authorized Version of 1611 has made us familiar. Miles Coverdale completed the work which Tyndale had begun. No book has had an equal influence on the English people. Apart from all religious considerations, it gave, to all classes alike, an idiom in which the deeper emotions of life could be recalled. It gave grace to the speech of the unlettered, and it entered into the style of the most ambitious writers. Its phrasing coloured the work of poets, and its language has so embedded itself in our national tradition that if the Bible is forgotten a precious possession will be lost.

The translation of the Bible was only the centre of a religious literature which in controversy and commentary bulked large in England from the sixteenth to the nineteenth century. Anyone who has been in an old library must sometimes have contemplated with mixed feelings the energies which have gone into the production of sermons, or into angry and learned argument on theology and Church government. Only a few of these writings have the strength in design, or the human interest in theme, to keep them alive. In the sixteenth century, of all works of this kind, John Foxe's (1516-87) *Acts and Monuments of these Latter and Perilous Days* (1563), popularly known as Foxe's *Book of Martyrs*, had the widest renown. Foxe had collected the details of the deaths of the Protestant martyrs, and these he relates with an impassioned fury at their fate. To the modern reader, Foxe's accumulation is so long that it becomes monotonous, though many of the individual accounts have still a human poignancy. For a century or more Foxe's volume was the great book of English Protestantism, and for many the only book, apart from the Bible, which they had read. Religious controversy in the sixteenth century produced one excellent prose writer in Richard Hooker (1554-1600), whose *Laws of Ecclesiastical Polity* began publication in 1594. Hooker arose above the heat of argument, and in a quiet, systematic way set down the principles on which the Church of England should be governed, discovering in its compromise only an evidence of its wisdom. As he found a middle road in religion, so he found a middle road in style, a path between the English and the Latin with the virtues of both, clarity and dignity, strengthened by a native harmony. In character he is an example of a man of great knowledge and wisdom, devoid of material ambition, content with a rural living, and undiverted by the company of a shrew from the task he had set himself. Had England listened to the voice of Hooker the centuries which followed would have been less embarrassed by internal conflict and controversy.

The sixteenth century had nothing in its prose to match the excellence of the drama, yet scholars had been preparing the way for the acceptance of English as the standard medium of expression. So Roger Ascham, the tutor of Lady Jane Grey, wished that England might be for learning and wisdom 'a spectacle to all the World beside,' and he attempted to carry out his aim in *Toxophilus* (1545), a dialogue on the art of archery, and in *The Schoolmaster* (1570). The ordinary life of England does not come much into Elizabethan prose, though, as has been seen, Robert Greene, Thomas Dekker, and the other novelists and pamphleteers show something of the English Autolycus in action. Translation, chronicle, and history still continue as the main work of prose. In 1579 Sir Thomas North published his version of Plutarch's *Lives of the Noble Grecians and Romans*, the most famous of all the Tudor translations because Shakespeare was content not only to employ its themes but its very phrases in his Roman plays, particularly in *Antony and Cleopatra* and *Coriolanus*. The Elizabethan translators, like some of the sailors of the time, were freebooters, and North translated not from the original, but from the French of Jacques Amyot. He employed also his own gift for happy and ingenious phrasing. Apart from North,

Shakespeare also used Philemon Holland's translation of Pliny's *Natural History*. This was an outline of the science of the ancient world, and included everything, from sober observation to winged beasts and monstrosities.

If translators made available the ancient world, the chroniclers laid bare the past of England, and the deeds of Englishmen everywhere. Shakespeare again has given a special importance to the name of Raphael Holinshed, whose *Chronicle* was the basis for the English historical plays. Holinshed worked with collaborators, and he cannot compete with North in the dignity and beauty of his language. But he had a great lucidity, and whatever his prejudices, he had a clear conception of his great theme and of the characters that played upon it. If Holinshed gives the background of England, Richard Hakluyt (1553-1616) gave the modern adventures and discoveries of his countrymen in *The Principal Voyages* (1589-1600). Hakluyt's aim was a practical one: he wished to find 'ample vents' for our manufactured goods, and to develop colonial possessions. His work is largely a compilation, made from the accounts of the voyagers themselves. When he writes himself, he has a strength, and even at times a haunting beauty in his sentences. Hakluyt had described the discovery of the geographical earth, but in the seventeenth century Robert Burton (1577-1640), in the strange but fascinating *Anatomy of Melancholy* (1621), explored the human mind with the aid of all the learning of the classical world. He is a freebooting scholar, who finds his prizes all equally worth while, and all equally relevant to the great purpose which he has in hand. He examines the disease of melancholy, Hamlet's disease, which was to those times what psycho-analysis has been to the twentieth century. Few volumes in English are so full of curiosities, and this eccentric writer has given pleasure to discerning minds in all the centuries since his death.

The great prose writer of the early seventeenth century is Francis Bacon (1561-1626), and it is not without significance that the middle of his career should coincide with the publication of the Authorized Version of the Bible. If the Bible gave religion its great document, Bacon encouraged the methods of scientific investigation, which later were to challenge Christian thought. Bacon himself is orthodox enough in his religious professions, but the attitude he encouraged came into conflict with faith, and indeed with any mystical view of human experience. Most of Bacon's work is in Latin, and it is ironical that the greatest prose writer of the time should have mistrusted the permanence of English as a language. Bacon is the most complete representative of the Renaissance in England, learned, worldly, ambitious, intriguing, enamoured of all the luxury that wealth in his times can supply, and while knowing so much, yet almost completely ignorant of his own nature. One can picture him in his study, in the half-light, with music playing softly in an adjoining room, running his fingers through a heap of precious stones, while his mind all the while contemplates the nature of truth. His *History of Henry the Seventh* gave historical writing in England the first work which had design. His unfinished narrative of the *New Atlantis* told an adventure story in simple prose, and, in the manner of H. G. Wells, embedded in the middle of it a plea for historical research. *The Advancement of Learning*, a portion of his great scientific work, described the condition of knowledge and the way in which it might be improved. None of these can equal in human interest the *Essays* (1597). The essays added in the editions of 1612 and 1625 are in each instance significant of different periods of Bacon's life. In 1597 with such essays as 'Of Studies,' Bacon informs the ambitious young man how he can make his way in the world. In 1612 he has a wider range of theme, and suggests the responsibilities of power. The third volume, with its essay 'Of Gardens,' hints at the release of retirement. The essays are compact in style, almost gnomic, with a pretty balance in the phrasing, and with images, such as, 'men fear death as children fear to go into the dark,' which have become part of the common tradition of our speech. In arrangement they are precise and well-ordered, as one expects from a scientist, though not always with equal success. In this they contrast with the happy and informal intimacy of Montaigne.

The first half of the seventeenth century was a period of

religious controversy, of Civil War, and of the triumph of Puritanism. The great monuments of its prose have solemnity and seriousness, and an impressive grandeur. The modern reader, who comes upon them for the first time, will feel a sense of remoteness, but he cannot easily fail to perceive a majesty, present in that age, which has never returned into the language. Prose was to discover itself in other ways, to become more pliable, more useful, even more human, but no one repeated the magnificent and sombre eloquence of Sir Thomas Browne, Jeremy Taylor, or John Milton.

Sir Thomas Browne (1605-82) was a physician, resident in Norwich, who lived through the Civil Wars but seemed entirely unaffected by them. He was learned in the science of his time, and he knew Bacon's methods of investigation. Not less he was attracted to religion, and he had read widely in classical and modern authors. He seems to stand, as does so much of the seventeenth century, midway between the modern and medieval ways of thought. Some of his science belongs to modern investigation, but he was seriously interested in popular superstitions, such as whether elephants have joints. He had a tolerance in religion, so that he could 'never hear the Ave-Mary bell without an elevation,' but he believed in witches, and his evidence sent some of these unfortunate women to their death. He had a longing for the incredible, and for the incidents in the Bible which are magical, though he knows how remote they are from the records of experience. This duality in his mind does not lead to fretfulness, though it may account for his gentle melancholy. He admires reason, but he sees that human life is part of a greater experience. Whatever his theme, he is conscious of the great spectre of death at the end of the road. It is unceasing awareness of death which informs his *Hydriotaphia, or Urn Burial* (1658), where his solemn prose rises to its most imaginative and majestic effects. More varied is his spiritual autobiography *Religio Medici* (published 1642), which he wrote before he was thirty. Seldom has English stretched itself to the harmonies which Browne controls in his long sentences, marshalled with words, many of them of Latin origin and all of them well-sounding. The age which produced

Sir Thomas Browne also possessed in Jeremy Taylor (1613-67) the most eloquent preacher that the English Church possessed. He is best remembered for his *Holy Living* (1650) and his *Holy Dying* (1651), but his sermons surpass these in the passion and splendour of their language.

The political controversies of the age drove John Milton to write in prose, that is to write, as he himself described it, with his left hand. Much of his most interesting prose was in Latin, his defence of the English people and his expression of his own very individual views on Christianity, the *De Doctrina Christiana*. The interest has fallen out of some of his English prose because its themes were ephemeral, such as his notions on divorce, and on Church Government. Two pamphlets will remain of importance: his defence of the encyclopaedic method in education, and his plea for free speech and writing in the *Areopagitica* (1644). Milton appeared at his best in this pamphlet where he expressed his finely founded belief in the rightness of the human spirit if left to develop unrestricted. As elsewhere, he voiced his love of England, or of what he hoped England might be; 'a noble and puissant nation rousing herself like a strong man after sleep, and shaking her invincible locks.' His prose does not read easily. He was so familiar with the Latin sentence, which with its inflexions can be well-ordered even when it is elaborate, that he forgot that English cannot contain a multitude of clauses in a single sentence without confusion. Nor must Latin be allowed to take the whole blame for his labyrinthine sentences: his own subtle mind immediately seized upon modifications for each statement that it conceived, so that a thought in Milton can be as encircled with limiting clauses as a section in the Finance Acts, and with the same detriment to immediate clarity. He had another side to his prose, for when heated in controversy he could exchange with an opponent strong, coarse terms, as was the fashion of the time. At its best, his prose rises above these complications, and above these defects, and, particularly in *Areopagitica*, an impassioned eloquence clarifies it into lucidity and power.

One writer stands apart from all these tendencies, and yet of all the prose authors of that age he has made the greatest appeal to posterity. Izaak Walton (1593-1683) published his *Compleat Angler* in 1653, and since then the volume has never lacked readers. Not less valuable are his lives of Donne, Hooker, George Herbert, and others, which he published in 1670. Walton had a long life, stretching from the Elizabethan Age to the Restoration, and his amiable optimism seems untouched by the troubles of his country in those years. His *Angler*, which coincides with the Civil War, is a gentle praise of his sport, and of the English countryside through which it leads him.

With the Restoration of 1660, English prose seems to make a new beginning. The Court had been to France and had learned there the virtues of clear writing, for which the French have been justly praised. Lucidity had never been absent from English prose, as the language of the Bible shows, but the ambitious writers, especially of the early seventeenth century, had aimed, not at lucidity, but at grandeur. The change comes, not from any deliberate imitation of French prose, but because English prose-writers attempt the easy, sociable sense which French prose possessed. Jeremy Taylor's prose is prose in party dress, or, if the metaphor is more acceptable, prose in canonicals; it will not do the tasks of a maid-of-all-work. Sir Thomas Browne's prose is prose of such a kind; it will not serve for conversation. The change can be exaggerated, for some Restoration writers are stiff and dull. The emotional temperature of prose declined, and this can be seen by comparing the sermons of Jeremy Taylor with those of Robert South or John Tillotson. Much of the interest of the age lay in science and philosophy, and these studies enacted from prose precision and bareness. While the Court was enjoying the comedies of Wycherley or Congreve, the Royal Society was being founded for the investigation of scientific problems. This spirit of enquiry extended, beyond science, into literature and philosophy. The scientists were seeking a bare and honest prose such as is described by Thomas Sprat in his *History of the Royal Society* (1667). John Dryden, poet and dramatist, applied himself in prose to examine the workshop of literature in essays, modelled on those of Corneille, of which *The Essay of*

Dramatic Poesy (1668) is the earliest, and *The Preface to the Fables* (1700), written in the year of his death, is the most engaging, especially in the comparison of Chaucer and Ovid. Dryden had some of the old mannerisms in his prose, but, at his best, he combined 'the other harmony of prose' with an easy manner of creating an informal atmosphere, and of allowing the reader to enter into the development of an argument.

The scientists deliberately encouraged simplicity, but the virtue had penalties, for the age has few works of the imagination, apart from John Bunyan's allegories, composed by a mind neither helped nor hindered by the tradition of his time. It is well that this economy and clarity coincided with the beginning of the most important period of English philosophy. Of these philosophers the most alarming was a timid man, Thomas Hobbes, who, born in 1588, contrived to cling to the existence which he was always afraid to lose until 1678. Hobbes suggested that human life, including thought, was the result of physical changes. Our senses received impressions, and we registered reactions to them, and that was the sum of experience and of morality. As we were all registering these reactions, the world would soon be reduced to a state of anarchy if there were not some control. Hobbes was a seventeenth-century totalitarian. But he was not a revolutionary who wished himself to be at the centre of power. That he discreetly reserved for his Stuart masters. In his *Leviathan* (1651), in which he relates his theories to politics, he makes it amply clear that the monarchy alone can preserve society from disruption.

Hobbes's extreme materialism was modified in the philosophy of John Locke (1632-1704), who developed a system in which knowledge was based on experience, but experience itself was not so closely related to physical reactions as in Hobbes. Locke's *An Essay Concerning Human Understanding* (1690) had a wide influence both on the Continent and in England. It is one of the greatest works of English philosophy, and one of the most typical of the English temperament. The abstract is held in a nice compromise with the concrete, and all is related to the test of experience. Both Hobbes and Locke write with clarity. Hobbes has a strange acrid beauty in his prose, and Locke has lucidity without charm.

The science of the time is interested in the human mind, and at the same time men become more interested in themselves, as can be seen in the diaries, the journals, and the histories which survive from this age. Before the Restoration, the individual voice is seldom heard, or, if it is heard, it is on some important or public occasion. But now, for the first time, there walks through English prose a man discussing the intimate details of his own life. He is not an ordinary man, but he writes of the things which the ordinary man has known. He wrote for himself, in secret, but his work has been transcribed, and so Samuel Pepys (1633-1703) has become the most famous prose-writer of the late seventeenth century. Even if Pepys had not kept a diary he would have been a great figure in the history of England, the founder of the Royal Navy, an outstanding Civil Servant, and a President of the Royal Society. In his diary, he revealed the other Pepys, privately for his own eye, and without shame, his pleasures and vanities, his philanderings, and the details of each passing day. Nothing in English literature can compare with this confession, and the human mind itself should gain some liberation from the way in which Pepys records himself.

Pre-eminent though Pepys was, there were others in his age who shared his interest in recording their own lives. Pepys's friend, John Evelyn (1620-1706), a fellow-member of the Royal Society, a courtier, and a country gentleman, kept an account of his more discreet existence. He was interested in gardens, in courts, in travel, in smoke-abatement, and in himself. Wealthy, cultivated, and widely travelled, he is a notable contrast to the conception of the licentious Restoration courtiers which the popular imagination gathers from the works of Rochester.

Pepys and Evelyn described their own lives, but when Edward Hyde, Earl of Clarendon (1609-74), came to write of himself he found that he had to write the history of England in his own time. He was one of Charles I's advisers, and he was in exile with Charles II until the Restoration, when he became Lord Chancellor. The later years of his life were spent in exile again. His *History of the Rebellion*, published in 1702, is the first work in England since Alfred's *Chronicle* in which great events are recorded by a man who was himself a central figure. Even if his style is not easy, it gives an impression of the great days through which he lived. Clarendon never came fully to terms with syntax, with the actual management of the sentence but he had a rare mastery of phrase.

The intimacy, which appeared in Restoration prose, lives on in the days of Queen Anne, the most sociable period of our literature. Much of the prose of the age goes into the novel, but some of the fiction writers were talented in other ways. Daniel Defoe, who is often remembered only for *Robinson Crusoe*, did much to establish English journalism, and in his paper, *The Review*, set the eighteenth century upon the genial task of composing the periodical paper. This employment developed with Sir Richard Steele (1672-1729), and Joseph Addison (1672-1719). Manners, fashions, literature, stories, moral reflections, all took a turn as themes in brief papers, which were addressed consciously to a middle-class audience. Both Steele and Addison came to understand precisely what was required, though Addison had to turn himself from a rather stiff and formal scholar into a man who could talk genially. The periodical essay was the eighteenth-century equivalent of the broadcast talk, and Addison found that a group of recognizable characters made his task easier. So he came to invent Sir Roger de Coverley, and the other members of the Spectator Club.

Steele and Addison wrote for their audiences, determined not to give offence. Jonathan Swift (1667-1745) wrote, without regard for any man, the vision of life as he saw it. The long list of his satires extends from *The Battle of the Books* and *A Tale of a Tub* (1704) to *Gulliver's Travels* (1726), and beyond, into the more bitter works of his last period. Swift has often been presented as a diseased misanthropist, who saw his fellow-men as the Yahoos of the fourth book of *Gulliver*. Little of this is true. Swift had a mind over-vexed by the inconvenience and inadequacies of the physical apparatus of the human body, of its uncleanliness and its odours, and of the absurdity of the sexual act, when it is considered methodically by a non-participant. But his *Journal to Stella* shows that his fellow-men liked him, and that to Esther Johnson, whom in many, if not all, senses of the word he loved, he could show a genuine affection. The *Drapier's Letters* (1724) reveal his hatred of political chicanery and his genuine understanding of the Irish people. Proud he may have been, and even arrogant, but this arose from the dread possession of a vision unlike that of ordinary men. His insight would not permit of any concealment, and *Gulliver*, apart from being a good story, is the indictment of the human race for refusing reason and benevolence as the ways of life. If he was arrogant in himself, he was modest in his philosophy, and would have man order his life without war, and without corruption, before he began more ambitious studies. It is typical of this modesty that his prose is clear, but it is a clarity sustained by the most vigorous mind of the century. It defies imitation. Never is the meaning obscure, and each argument is developed with a deadly certainty, not through rhetoric, but by putting the proper words in the proper places.

CHAPTER THIRTEEN

MODERN ENGLISH PROSE

IN the eighteenth century the subjects of study to which man applied himself became more numerous and more systematic and it was the good fortune of England that prose in that age had become a pliant and serviceable medium. It was a century full of speculation and fierce questioning, a century with powerful minds that applied themselves to the problems of the nature of life, and set out solutions which have been the basis of much later thought. It was a century, above all others, when England led Europe in philosophical speculation. The centre of interest was human experience, and what could be learned from it of the nature of life, and here the eighteenth century looked back to Locke, if not always for guidance, at least for its terms of reference. Richardson and Fielding explored human experience in fiction. Historians were attempting, more ambitiously than before, to interpret the past of life, and philosophers to expound the nature of reality itself. It was natural that in such a century the orthodox teachings of the Church should be open to criticism, and it was fortunate for the Church that in Joseph Butler (1692-1752) it found its ideal exponent. In his lucid work, *The Analogy of Religion* (1736), he attempted to find the justification for religion out of such limited knowledge as experience itself supplies.

Among the sceptical minds produced by the century none is more original than Bernard Mandeville (1670-1733). In *The Fable of the Bees* (1714) he exposes the difference between private morality and the morality of states, suggesting, in an ironical manner, that the more corrupt a state is the more successful it will be. Though Mandeville has superficial disguises to preserve his mental respectability, his underlying intentions are clear, and much in his work reads like a modern condemnation of commerce and governments.

George Berkeley (1685-1753), like Mandeville, saw life as corrupt, but he approached the problem, not with irony, but with a generous and idealistic desire for reform, which led him to attempt a campaign among the settlers and the natives in America. While thus concerned with the practical side of life, he brought to the problems of philosophy one of the most acute minds of the age. In a series of volumes beginning with *An Essay Towards a New Theory of Vision* (1709), he expounded in a clear prose the theory that the material world does not exist, and that human knowledge is based on the ideas within the mind. While materialism was increasing man's attachment to the concrete world, Berkeley reasserted an idealism which, though closely argued, has in it strong elements of mysticism. David Hume (1711-76) also attached his mind to the problem of knowledge, but with conclusions which seems to remove the unity which Berkeley achieved. He pursued the psychological studies of Descartes and Locke into the nature of human thinking, only to discover that the human mind, as an instrument for elucidating truth, is inadequate. The scepticism of his *Essays Concerning Human Understanding* (1748) has left a mark on human thought which has been permanent. Each branch of human knowledge has had to speak less complacently of its assertions since Hume wrote.

Hume was himself an historian, and the spirit of enquiry of the age led others to investigate the human past in a systematic way. The art of history, in this important period of its development, was fortunate in attracting one who was a master of English prose. Edward Gibbon (1737-94) began the publication of *The Decline and Fall of the Roman Empire* in 1776. A moving passage in his *Autobiography* records the completion of the great work in 1788. His theme was no less than the break-up of the ancient world and the establishment of modern civilization; from Rome in the second century to its capture by the Barbarians, to the enthronement of Charlemagne and the establishment of the Holy Roman Empire in the west, and then forward through the Middle Ages to the capture of Constantinople by the Turks in 1453. The impression made on the reader is one of unity, and of design. Gibbon had a mind powerful to control the wide areas he had to describe, a thoroughness in preparation, and a skill in prose that gives to almost any sentence a delight, even when it is detached from its context. It was style that ultimately gave the work its unity, for it carried him safely over the barren places. At the centre of his work lay the story of Christianity, and, towards religion as a whole Gibbon was sceptical. He had the added dilemma that, for the middle sections of his work, it was upon the Catholic historians that he had to rely. One feels that his own religious education had wounded him, and that he revenges himself with irony and innuendo; so in his account of monasticism he writes: 'Egypt, the fruitful parent of superstition, afforded the first example of the monastic life'; and such examples are numerous. This hostility to Christianity gave to the centre of his history an emptiness, which only the unvarying excellence of his style conceals. In compensation, he had aloofness and detachment, and an honesty in examining all the sources available. He had a very modest belief in human nature, and very little faith in progress, and so, in the age when Rousseau was writing, and England was losing the American Colonies, he turned back to the decay of that classical world, which to him had come as near to an image of perfection as human life was likely to afford.

Among Gibbon's friends was Dr Samuel Johnson (1709-84). His powerful personality, and his long literary career, made him the dominating literary figure of the century. His reputation owes much to the art of James Boswell (1740-95), whose *Life of Johnson* was published in 1791. He has portrayed the Johnson of the later years, from minute records of his sayings, and his mannerisms, and with a realistic art that has no parallel. The capacity, the wit, and the downrightness of Johnson, along with his often kindly and always devout appraoch to life, are the elements of the portrait which Boswell has created, and without his biographer Johnson would be a lesser man. He would still occupy a foremost place in the literature of his age. Part of his contribution belonged to those systematic studies for which the century is famous. His edition of Shakespeare (1765) helped in the eighteenth-century task of interpreting the text of the plays, and one can often find clarity in Johnson where other editors remain obscure. The *Preface* to this edition, a brave piece of criticism, finally rescued the plays from the more pedantic judgments of neo-classic criticism. His central work, and nowhere is the clarity of his mind seen more firmly, was the *Dictionary* (1747-55), upon which all later lexicographical studies have been based. The definition of words is one of the stiffest tasks to which a human mind can apply itself, and it is regrettable that Johnson is sometimes remembered for the few satiric definitions that he inserted by way of relaxation. No one has equalled him in describing clearly to the English people what the words in their language really mean. To these great achievements he added, in his later years, *The Lives of the Poets* (1779-81), in which, in a prose that often matches his conversation, he gives an account of English poetry from Cowley to Gray. Nothing in Johnson can compare with these three great monuments of his massive intelligence. His *Rasselas* has already been mentioned in the history of fiction. In *The Rambler* and *The Idler* he applied himself to the periodical paper, and introduced into his essays a deeper moral gravity than Addison practised. His wisdom, his prejudices, and the range of his interests are nowhere better seen than in *A Journey to the Western Islands of Scotland* (1775).

No figure in the century lives so clearly in the imagination, though it must always be remembered that Boswell's picture is of the old and leisured man. The attraction of his personality should not diminish the solid merit of his literary lexicographical labours. His style has an elegance that depends on balance, and is unjustly remembered by the few more ponderous phrases that are sometimes quoted against him. He was English in his strength and his weakness; pious, suspicious of mysticism, conservative, proud of his downrightness, but with a tender heart. Clarity he valued above the 'finer shades,' and morality he valued above art. If some of his literary opinions seem odd, it is only because he was never insincere in his assignment of praise and blame. In his prose, and in his verse, he was a classicist, but he was a classicist who had the clear sight and brave judgment to set Shakespeare in his right place amid the dramatists, though one suspects that part of his pleasure in doing so came from the knowledge that he was disagreeing with Voltaire.

Compared with Johnson the mind of Oliver Goldsmith (1730-74) seems puny and inadequate, but in creative talent Goldsmith was more richly endowed. As Johnson said of him in an epitaph, he attempted every type of literature and each type he attempted he adorned. His dramas and his novel have already been recorded, and his hack-work of history is best left without record. His essays, however, showed his individuality, and in *The Citizen of the World* (1762) he comments on life through the imaginary letters of a Chinese visitor.

The variety of Johnson's circle can be seen by the fact that it included not only Oliver Goldsmith, the impoverished writer, who economically never escaped from Grub Street, but Edmund Burke (1729-97), who stood high in the councils of the nation. Apart from an early treatise on aesthetics, *The Sublime and Beautiful* (1756), and his editorship of *The Annual Register*. Burke's main work is to be found in a series of political pamphlets, mainly delivered in the form of speeches. On two major issues he expressed himself with emphasis. He opposed the Government in its attitude to the revolting American colonists in *On American Taxation* (1774), and *On Conciliation with America* (1775). With even more vehemence he attacked the French Revolution, notably in his *Reflections on the French Revolution* (1790). In these, and in a number of speeches, including his attack on Warren Hastings, the body of his prose and his political doctrine is to be found.

Burke's oratory becomes a part of English history. He has to undergo a change of thought which looks like inconsistency. In defending the American colonists he seems to be defending freedom, and in opposing the French Revolution he appears to be on the side of tyranny. Actually, there is no change, but an inner consistency. Burke was opposed to abstract theory. The French Revolution was to him a dangerous experiment in bringing a theoretical philosophy into practice. The Government's attitude to the American colonists seemed also to be an attempt to impose 'metaphysical' claims upon them. Burke, like so many others in his century, based his thought on experience. The first law of society was man's relation to God, and the image of that law was to be found, not in paper-made theories, but in custom and tradition. Burke is the great exponent of Conservatism, for while he relies on experience, he will not trust solely to the reason, because he finds that experience itself is not governed by the reason. Burke in his prose always has the spoken word in mind, and though he argues closely, he has the audience in view. This contact with the audience gives him the eloquence and the passion which enter into some of his best-known passages. He is freer in his effects than Johnson or Gibbon, and, at times, he would introduce phrases which Johnson thought too familiar. These vary a style whose main effect is an ornate and rich movement, though never beyond the control of the informing mind.

Much that is most attractive in the prose of the eighteenth century goes into the private letters and journals of an age that had the leisure and cultivation to make correspondence a fine art. Thomas Gray, whose poetical production is slender and impersonal, reveals, in his letters, his 'white' melancholy and a mind as learned in literature as any in his age in Europe. William Cowper is more lively in his letters, than in his poems. He captures all the details and oddities of everyday life into his amusing descriptions. John Wesley (1703-91), the founder of Methodism, in his diary gives a vivid and human account of the movement for which he struggled. Horace Walpole (1717-97) exercised all his wit and observation to make his vast collection of letters a memorial of eighteenth-century life. An even more accomplished art is to be found in the letters of the Earl of Chesterfield (1694-1773) to his illegitimate son, Philip Stanhope. A nobleman of the older school, he sets out, in deliberate and epigrammatic phrases, the philosophy that treasures good manners and the arts of pleasing, and distrusts enthusiasm, and sentimentality, or any form of boisterousness. To read Chesterfield and Wesley together is to see how varied were the ways of thought that the eighteenth century pursued. In reading the letters of Walpole, one can realize that the eighteenth century had longings for some world of mystery, beyond the elegant drawing-rooms in which so many of Chesterfield's days were spent. Some of that desire was satisfied by James Macpherson (1736-96), in a series of narratives, known collectively as *The Works of Ossian.* Macpherson is one of the most pathetic figures in our literature. With some knowledge of Gaelic traditions, he invented in a rhythmical prose a number of narratives which he alleged to be translations of early poems. As such they were accepted by many strong minds, but when their authenticity was questioned, Macpherson had to sit down and try to invent the originals of his own invention. He answered strongly to some need in his age, and not in England alone, for the sombre and vague grandeur of his narratives attracted Goethe and Napoleon. Had he been content to come forward as an original and creative writer, his own career would have been less troublesome, and he would still remain a formative influence in his age. He was answering the same need which in verse was satisfied by Thomas Percy's (1729-1811) collection of early ballads and poems, known as the *Reliques of English Poetry* (1765).

The main energies of romanticism in the early nineteenth century went into verse and the novel, but a new prose develops at the same time. S. T. Coleridge gave to literary criticism a deeper and more philosophical interpretation, both in his lectures and in the *Biographia Literaria* (1817). His original mind also conceived a more subtle and revealing vocabulary for criticism. If his philosophy is, in expression, fragmentary, his conception that faith depends on an active will to believe obviously influenced nineteenth-century thought. His letters are less effective than those of Keats, who seldom writes without falling intuitively upon some enlightening critical thought, and who expresses, without affectation, the ever-quickened development of his own genius. Coleridge's place as a thinker still remains to be estimated for much of his miscellaneous writings are unpublished. In human interest, nothing in the period equals the letters and journals of Byron, who mingles wit with description, and a gay and indiscreet exposure of himself to his friends, with a reckless commentary on life and on his own times.

All these writers are remembered mainly for their verse, but Charles Lamb (1775-1834) has endeared himself to generations of Englishmen for his *Essays of Elia* (1823) and *Last Essays* (1833). Lamb belongs to the intimate and self-revealing essayists, of whom Montaigne is the original, and Cowley the first exponent in England. To the informality of Cowley he adds the solemn confessional manner of Sir Thomas Browne. In style, he makes an intricate mosaic of earlier writers, particularly those who affected the grand manner. This elaboration he uses in a gently humorous way, amid the sentiments and trifles of every day. To understand his personality and his intention is not so simple as may at first appear. Is 'Elia,' the sentimental, smiling figure of the essays, really Lamb or only a cloak with which Lamb hides himself from the world? He understood the great things in the literature of his time, the poems of Wordsworth and Coleridge, and in criticism he has a sympathy for the harrowing moments in literature. He can criticize *King Lear* with understanding, but when he comes to write himself, he composes a dissertation on roast pork. It may be that a solution can be found on that September evening in 1796, when his sister Mary, in a fit of insanity, stabbed her mother to death, and wounded her father. Lamb devoted his life to the care of his sister, and the part of his mind which was creative could not face tragedy, though he could understand tragedy when he found it in the works of others. So in the essays he plays with trivialities, though as Walter Pater has said, 'we know that beneath this blithe surface there is something of the domestic horror, of the beautiful heroism, and devotedness too, of old Greek tragedy.'

One of the best-known figures in Lamb's circle of friends was William Hazlitt (1778-1830), whose essays still read with some of their original freshness. Part of Hazlitt's training had been as a painter, and he uses words as if he enjoyed their colour. In his numerous essays he is always downright in his opinions, and he uses pungent and illuminating phrases to reveal his judgments. As a personality he is as difficult as Lamb is kindly. There is a violence in his judgments, not only in his hates, but in his attachments. Though he is a Radical, he believes in Napoleon, and he spends his last years struggling to write a life of Napoleon. The effect of his personality on his own life can be seen in *Liber Amoris* (1823), where he appears as a Rousseau with a sense of irony. Of his many volumes of essays the most effective is *The Spirit of the Age* (1825), in which he gives critical portraits of most of his contemporaries.

As a critic Thomas de Quincey (1785-1859) is less reliable than Hazlitt, but in the *Confessions of an English Opium Eater* (1821) he brought into prose a new accent. He describes his experiences and his dreams as an opium addict, and for the dream descriptions he employs a 'poetic prose,' elaborate and sonorous in its effects. In refreshing contrast is the prose of William Cobbett (1763-1835). He wrote voluminously, breezily, often pugnaciously, and he had a natural gift for exciting the reader in his experiences and his views. Of all his works, *Rural Rides* (1830), which describes his journeys on horseback through England, is the most effective. He shows the counties as they were, with a quick eye for detail, especially for a 'field full of turnips,' and there is often an unaffected beauty in his descriptions. While Cobbett will always find readers wherever his works circulate, opinion is more likely to differ on the merits of Walter Savage Landor (1775-1864). His tempestuous and eccentric personality separated him from his contemporaries, and it has kept both his verse and his prose apart from the tradition of literature in his age. His prose is certainly far more readable than his poetry, and the *Imaginary Conversations* (1824-9) show the range of his knowledge, and the beauty which he could command from words.

Throughout the nineteenth century there was an audience for solid periodicals and reviews. Though these were organized mainly on a political basis, they devoted ample space to the criticism of literature. The longest lived of these journals was *The Gentleman's Magazine* (1731-1868), which continued in existence from the age of Pope to the age of Browning. In the first decade of the nineteenth century the great political journals began circulation with *The Edinburgh Review*. The most powerful of all such periodicals, it had as editor Francis Jeffrey (1773-1850), who as a literary critic exercised his talents in demolishing the romantic poets. One of its most brilliant contributors was Sydney Smith (1771-1845), whose mind is satiric but witty. He is frequently prejudiced, but like Dr Johnson he can give the impression of a monopoly in common sense. Sometimes he is reminiscent of Swift, and sometimes of Macaulay, but he is more genial than either in the careless exuberance of his wit. *The Quarterly Review* (1809) began publication as a Tory answer to the *Edinburgh*, and Scott was for a time one of its contributors. It was followed by *Blackwood's Edinburgh Magazine*, in which J. G. Lockhart, Scott's son-in-law and biographer, was a leading spirit and one of the most virulent of contributors. *Blackwood's* is often remembered only for its scurrilous attacks on Keats, but this is unjust, for it contained much lively writing, including John Wilson's *Noctes Ambrosianae*, written under the name of 'Christopher North.' All these reviews showed the presence of an alert and educated public which was prepared to exercise its mind, and such a public continued to exist throughout the nineteenth century.

Literary production in the nineteenth century is so voluminous and varied, that only the works which have a fresh approach to prose can be considered. This is less unjust than it may seem, for only in Charles Darwin did the century possess a thinker of the importance of Hume or Burke. Charles Darwin (1809-82) would have disclaimed any right to be considered as a literary artist, yet the clarity of his style, and the very quietness with which he presents his profound conclusions, give to much of his work the qualities of a work of art. In *The Origin of Species* (1859), and in *The Descent of Man* (1871), he brought to light conceptions of the origins of man which challenged orthodox religion and accepted opinion everywhere. His own investigations and conclusions he had stated with great caution, and in this lies much of his artistry, but the consequences of his thought could not be avoided, and they were emphasized in the clear, insistent prose of T. H. Huxley (1825-95).

Both Darwin and Huxley were more effective as writers of prose than the political philosophers of the early part of the century. As thinkers, the radical philosophers have their own importance, for they developed the twin conceptions of individuality and *laissez-faire*, which are behind so much English thought in the nineteenth century. As literature, their work is less attractive. Jeremy Bentham (1748-1832) writes clearly, and one can appreciate the mind controlling the complexity of the material, but there the attraction ends. Similarly one can go to T. R. Malthus for his ideas on population, but not for aesthetic pleasure. The same is true of James Mill, and in style the work of John Stuart Mill (1806-73) is far more attractive, especially in his *Autobiography*.

The glamour, which the philosophers of politics lacked, was found in full measure in the prose of Thomas Babington Macaulay (1800-59). He brought to the composition of his essays a mind that was richly stored with detail, and brutally clear in its convictions. This allowed him to set forth his theme with a simplicity that avoided every compromise, and this firm outline, once defined, he decorated with every embellishment of allusion and picturesque detail. Such a method he followed in his studies of Bacon, Johnson, and Warren Hastings, and it serves admirably as long as the first, simple formula is sound. Brilliant though the essays may be, they do not compare in solid worth with the *History of England* (1849-61). Though sometimes dismissed as a mere justification of Whig policy, this work has security and design combined with Macaulay's unsurpassed use of detail. In no earlier work had the life of England been made to live so clearly, and though Macaulay had no predecessors, he may have gained something from Scott's imaginative treatment of the past and from Gibbon's mastery of form.

The nineteenth century was to produce many historians, Froude, Lecky, Hallam, and others, but the most original was Thomas Carlyle (1795-1882), who used history only as one of the methods of his teaching, but always used it honestly. He addressed himself to his age in a long series of volumes, of which the most impressive were *Sartor Resartus* (1833-4), *On Heroes and Hero-worship* (1841), *Past and Present* (1843). He also composed a series of historical studies of which the earliest, the *French Revolution*, gained him his reputation in 1837. The reader is affected by the style even before the thought can make its impression. The sentences come cascading forth, tumbling and spluttering, as if the very words were in a fury with the world. The effect varies from a comic irony to genuine eloquence, and Carlyle has added to his native gifts by a study of prose writers such as Sterne, and Fichte, the German philosopher, both of whom attempt ever to startle the reader with their language. Carlyle, in his prose, is attempting to stir his age from its complacency. He possesses a strange, unformulated mysticism which distrusts the reason and above all opposes the materialism of the Utilitarians. For him, the individual is the centre of life, and, as he shows in *Sartor Resartus*, the individual must overcome his hesitations and doubts, and affirm himself in faith and activity. Only thus can the corruption of society be checked, and he discovers in the individual at his highest the mystical figure of the 'hero.' Preacher though he may be, Carlyle is also an historian, and one who will not corrupt the evidence merely to support a case. He had learned from romanticism the way in which the past could be made to live, vivid in its detail, and this he achieved in his studies of the French Revolution, and of Cromwell, and less successfully in his long work on Frederick the Great. Today one may approach his teaching with reservations, for we have seen the romantic anti-intellectual in action in many unpleasant ways. But each age needs its own prophets, and, to the nineteenth century, Carlyle had a message that life could not be governed mechanically, or solely by reference to the audited accounts of a nation.

Carlyle tried to lead England back to a more spiritual life by a self-conceived doctrine. It was the same urge, working through a different channel, that led others, through the Oxford Movement, to a new movement in the English Church, and in some instances to Roman Catholicism. At once the most attractive personality in the group, and the most distinguished prose writer, was John Henry Newman (1801-90). He recounts his own spiritual history, in a most moving manner, in his *Apologia pro Vita Sua* (1864): the whole complexity of his personality is only now being realised with the publication of biographical materials. He was the master of a supple prose, dignified but resilient, and his mind, though moved by emotion, was disciplined by a fine intellect. These qualities allowed him to convey to his conversion to Roman Catholicism a human quality which gives a permanent attraction to his record.

Of all the writers who felt that the nineteenth century was inadequate, John Ruskin (1819-1900) expressed himself most voluminously. In *Modern Painters* (1843-60) he championed the art of Turner, and constructed a philosophy of the aesthetic which, in his mind, is almost a substitute for religion. In *The Seven Lamps of Architecture* (1849), and in *The Stones of Venice* (1851-3), he expounded the principles of architecture and eulogized the Gothic, to a generation that sadly misinterpreted his lessons. The arts led him to the craftsmen who are responsible for them, and this, in turn, directed his attention to the shabby commercialism of his age, which he attacked in *Unto this Last* (1862). Among his later and more informal works, were his letters to working men entitled *Fors Clavigera* (1871-87), and his autobiography, *Praeterita* (1885-9). Much that Ruskin said has now lost its urgency, and he himself changed his mind frequently in his own lifetime, but his central theme remains. Against the shabby mass productions of a mechanical age he set the work of craftsmen, who saw that each thing they made was well made, and beautifully made. He challenged, at least by implication, the whole basis on which a commercial society rests, and his influence lived on in William Morris (reference to whose prose was made when his poetry was considered), and in numerous other less well-known followers. With all his strength and vision, Ruskin had in him some element of weakness. To read his work is to listen to someone shouting continuously, and so loudly that one is distracted from the argument. It is true that his prose could at times assume the garments of magnificence, but even at their grandest the reader feels that the effects have been produced to overawe him. The quieter manner of his autobiography is a relief from the rhetoric of some of the earlier volumes.

To the criticism of England in the nineteenth century Matthew Arnold (1822-88) brought all the resources of his powerful intellect. He sees the English as a nation of 'Philistines,' dominated by a narrow dogma in religion, a petrified code of morality in conduct, and with a complete shallowness of literary taste. His attack is not carried to its logical conclusions, and varies in value. On religion, his own views have a gloomy morbidity, but when he speaks of literature he attempts, for the first time in the century, to evolve standards by which works of art can be judged. Against the insularity of his age, he brings a European outlook, and his style, with its happy gift of definition and for the invention of just but memorable phrases, gives an added attraction to his thought.

Among those who had studied Ruskin was Walter Pater (1839-94), though he studied him only to draw his own conclusions. While Ruskin had made art a religion, Pater made it an end in itself. In the *Conclusion* to *Studies in the History of the Renaissance* (1873), in a prose of a rare beauty, he set out his faith that the pursuit of beauty, whether in experience, or in works of art, was the most satisfactory activity that life offered. This quest of the most profitable experience he explored in the form of a novel in *Marius the Epicurean* (1885). His own sensitive appreciation of literature, and the other arts, he showed in a series of essays which seem to recreate the originals of which he speaks. The limitations of his philosophy are only too obvious, for he rejects all social and moral obligations, but the prose in which he describes his outlook combines precision of statement with a strange and compelling charm. The great prose writers of the nineteenth century from Carlyle to Arnold and Ruskin had been concerned with the problems of their age. These problems Pater rejects, just as in poetry they had been rejected by the pre-Raphaelites, and so with Pater the prose of the nineteenth century may be said to have come to an end.

The most interesting developments in contemporary prose are to be found in the drama and in fiction, in G. B. Shaw and in Joyce. The rest of the prose of the age is too voluminous for any brief summary to be of value. Nor is it possible as yet to distinguish the talents of the many competent writers who have added something to the tradition of the English language. Occasionally a writer such as G. K. Chesterton seems to be forcing prose into new effects, as if he were using his style as an advertisement for his thought. He seems like a poet corrupted by living in an age of advertisement, though something of the poet remains. It may be found that the less boisterous freshness of Hilaire Belloc will wear better, and many may turn to his essays to read of Europe as he saw it a few decades ago. A greater artistic security can be found in Sir Max Beerbohm's essays, which still reveal an eighteenth-century wit, bright and untarnished. As the century has gone on, we have for obvious reasons become distrustful of oratory, and the standard of our rhetoric has declined. To read today the early speeches of Lloyd George is to step into another world. The radio has made 'crooners' of us all; Winston Churchill alone retains the grand manner, and some of his eloquence will enter into what is permanent in our literature. He knows how to assert the colloquial phrase into the middle of a rhetorical paragraph, and despite all his great command of far-ranging resources of words, gestures caught from current idiom ('some chicken, some neck') are among his greatest national achievements. For the decline of rhetoric we have had the compensation of an increase in exposition and argument, to which the scientists have worthily contributed. The level of our newspaper prose has been improved far above any popular estimate. Despite some vulgarity, even the popular Press is written today with an alertness and an intelligence which make much of the journalism of thirty years ago seem archaic. Such a statement is bound to be disputed, but one has only to turn to the 'leaders' in the first issues of the *Daily Mail* and to compare them with the journalism of today to see how much the contemporary journalist is maligned.

While it is thus difficult to make any final estimate, one prose writer of the century stands a secure and supreme artist. Lytton Strachey (1880-1932), in his *Eminent Victorians* (1918), *Queen Victoria* (1921), and *Elizabeth and Essex* (1928) has given a new method in biography to which none of his imitators have approached. He broke through the tradition of the 'pious' biography of the nineteenth century, searching out for truth with a persistence which at first was over-weighted with the satirical. He belonged to a disillusioned age in which events seemed greater than men, and he turned upon the past in revenge to undermine its legend of the heroic. In an early study of French literature he had shown his admiration for Voltaire and a mood of eighteenth-century wit and rationalism informs him. In *Queen Victoria* he found a greater theme, and handled it with more balance. All that is incongruous in the Victorian age he exposed, and its insincerity he condemned with the most quiet but piercing of innuendoes. But he gave to the work a design as finished as in a portrait, and if he is sceptical of all that is false and pretentious, he comes at length to do justice to the ageing queen in pages which are not without pathos. His treatment of material is not always as honest as his prose but in the economy of his effects he is with Swift, and to be with Swift is to be with one of the best things that English prose in its long tradition of over a thousand years has produced.

INDEX